*In Search
of a Corporate Soul*

Other books by Roger M. D'Aprix

STRUGGLE FOR IDENTITY: THE SILENT REVOLUTION
AGAINST CORPORATE CONFORMITY

HOW'S THAT AGAIN? A GUIDE TO EFFECTIVE WRITTEN
AND ORAL COMMUNICATION IN BUSINESS

In Search
of a Corporate Soul

ROGER M. D'APRIX

The Presidents Association

Library of Congress Cataloging in Publication Data

D'Aprix, Roger M
    In search of a corporate soul

    Includes bibliographical references.
    1. Industry--Social aspects--United States.
2. Corporations--United States. 3. Industrial organi-
zation--United States. 4. Personnel management--
United States. I. Title.
HD60.5.U5D34   658.4   75-33364
ISBN 0-8144-5409-7

© *1976 AMACOM*
A division of American Management Associations, New York.
All rights reserved. Printed in the United States of America.

First Printing

For my children
Cynthia, Richard, Laura, and *Tony*
in the profound hope that each of you
will make some small difference
in a future world I can only contemplate
with a mixture of optimism and misgiving.
May the Lord be with each of you always
as you try to make that difference
in His name.

Acknowledgments

FOR the last several years I have held a management position with Xerox. It is an unusual corporation—perhaps even a unique one—and deserves the high public esteem in which it is regarded. I consider myself fortunate to be part of this company which, more than any other I've ever been associated with, has sought its own soul and has demonstrated some of the possibilities I've outlined in these pages. For anyone to have hope, he must see some possibility of progress and reform. Xerox has largely been the source of my own belief in the possibility of responsible corporate behavior.

Having said that, let me quickly add that none of the material in this book should be construed in any way, shape, or form to have the endorsement of Xerox. It is my own view of corporate life as I have known and observed it in a number of companies. I take responsibility for the book as a personal statement. The insights—both good and bad—are my insights. If there are flaws in the reasoning, if there are errors or omissions, they too are mine.

Besides the enlightenment of my employer, I also gratefully acknowledge the help of two of my co-workers in editing, typing, and checking the manuscript. The work of Elton L. Francis in keeping me as intellectually honest as I am capable of being is deeply appreciated. Cheryl Yehl's clerical assistance and attention to detail has been invaluable. Whatever errors or illogic remains in the text is the product of my not listening to their criticism or of my own lack of attention to detail.

And finally I reserve my greatest debt of gratitude for my wife, who tolerated my distraction, inattention, and general preoccupation as I lived through the gestation and delivery of this thing. Thank you for understanding.

Roger M. D'Aprix

Contents

CONTENTS

x

They [corporations] cannot commit treason, nor be outlawed nor excommunicate, for they have no souls.
Sir Edward Coke (1552–1634)
Case of *Sutton's Hospital*, 1612

. . . The world was left unfinished so that man might share in creation, redeeming the world from chaos. As man assumes responsibility for the world he humanizes it, for the world has no freedom or consciousness except in man. It is through the world that man becomes all he must be; it is through man that the world finds its place before God.
Anthony Padovano (1934–   )
Who Is Christ?

Introduction

A TRUISM about American society in the final third of
the twentieth century is that almost every speck of it
has been assigned to one organization or another. Whatever work we Americans do and almost regardless of
where we live, it is close to impossible to escape contact
with some kind of formal, and usually bureaucratic,
organization.

Bigness and concentration are more and more typical. This is true of government, it is true of education,
and it certainly is true of our economy. More and more
we deal with each other through complex and inflexible
systems which have neither the capacity nor the inclination to worry about us as individual personalities.

In the 1970s, organizations are not merely a fact of
life. They have become for most of us a way of life.
Unfortunately, we have not taken much time to try to
understand this way of life. Instead we are content to

live with the myths, the conventional wisdom, and the cynicism that have grown up around these complex institutions we have created and which now tend to dominate our lives.

Many Americans feel today as though they were on a speeding roller coaster, plummeting down the sharp slopes and then inching their way briefly to the next precipice to plunge once more. That's the way their work life feels. That's the way their relationships with many of our social and economic institutions feel. And that's often even the way their family relationships feel.

The helplessness that goes with this roller coaster ride seems to have led to a collective depression of the spirit, a weariness which hangs oppressively over our country in the 1970s. As I see it, we desperately need to regain some sense of control over our lives if we are to have any hope of shaking off the apprehension and the helplessness which are holding us captive.

This book deals with a special portion of that larger issue. It is a discussion of what is ailing our corporate organizations and how we might begin to renew them by making them more responsive to human needs and by giving them a human orientation—the task I call the search for a corporate soul. My experience tells me that significant numbers of people are coming to believe that institutional renewal of any kind is so frustrating and so bewildering that it's either futile or not worth the personal pain. Their answer is either to drift with the tide or to do their best to turn inward on their own lives and problems.

If they are right (and I believe most emphatically

that they are not), then twentieth-century man has rendered himself personally irrelevant and hopeless through the construction of his organizations.

That may sound like too somber a conclusion. I don't think so. I believe that if we turn our backs on the task of institutional reform in this highly organized society, we are digging our own graves. Our best hope—our only hope—is for each one of us to dedicate himself or herself to the frustrating and never-ending task of reforming and renewing our organizations to make them fit for human habitation, and to direct them in such a way that they make their human resources productive in doing the work society needs to have done.

Much of what has been written about that task has been stated in impersonal and analytical terms. We hear about new modes of organization. We hear about new management techniques. We hear seemingly endless discussions about management style. We hear about new planning systems. We hear about all sorts of schemes for dealing with the system and its shortcomings. But we need more than patchwork schemes, as effective and important as some of them may be.

What we need more than anything else is a new confidence which recognizes that individually and collectively we *can* renew and humanize the system. What we need is the firm conviction that the system must ultimately be made responsive to human needs so that each person can contribute in a productive way to meaningful work.

Some will read that to mean I am arguing that management should be kind to people. Though I happen to believe that as a tenet of simple human decency, this book is not an extended argument in support of better human relations in business. Most people who are in a position to help change unhealthy business environments are either impervious to such pleas or they see them as irrelevant to the more pressing short-term issues of efficiency, expediency, or earnings.

Thus anyone who argues for people orientation for its own sake—while certainly on the side of the angels—is mounting an argument which is destined to be largely ignored. That is particularly so when we are on the downside of a business cycle, as we are in the mid-1970s. At such a time, survival instincts override practically all other considerations, and cost effectiveness becomes the criterion for practically any business decision—including human relations.

So, for the record, this is not a book about the value of kindness in lubricating the business machine. Instead, it is a plea to all those who work and live within an organization to reflect on our common condition at this writing and to determine what we need to do together to make that organization habitable and productive.

In my view what is called for above all is a change in our own attitudes and perceptions so that we believe in the *possibility* of reform and so that we make a personal *commitment* to tidy up our own corners of the universe because that's obviously the only way we can begin.

In an earlier book, *Struggle for Identity,* I explored the issue of how an individual could protect himself against an unfeeling system. Here I have concerned myself with the much broader question of how the organization can humanize and update itself to function successfully in the 1970s and beyond. In that regard I have focused particularly on the role of the individual in working within the organization for effective change.

Those are the two subjects this book is about. I think they are also what the rest of our lives must be about.

CHAPTER I

The American Corporation: Dogma and Turmoil

A Perspective

THE first major premise of this book is a very simple one: Although American society has changed drastically —even convulsively—in the last 25 to 50 years, one of its fundamental institutions, the large business organization, has not kept up with the changes.

That lag is not surprising. Institutions in general never have been very good in responding to rapid-fire change. Most of them, in fact, tend to raise the drawbridge and double the castle guard when Change intrudes her unwelcome presence. While corporate and other institutional leaders usually make a great public display of courting Change and accommodating to her wishes, secretly they long for her to stop upsetting their older relationships. In truth they are more frightened than stimulated by her flirtations.

Usually with some bravado, managers cry that change is indeed good, that they believe in it and are doing everything possible to make their organizations responsive to the times; yet a great many of them go on managing their people and their resources as though it were 1950—or even 1935.

This sort of discrepancy is a curious and maddening phenomenon that has been identified by more astute observers than I. Still, a good many people in and out of business refuse to believe there is a problem. The facade of most large business organizations is so imposing and apparently so solid that people conclude that, while the structure may have a few creaking joints here and there, there's certainly no need for any rebuilding program. In truth, that facade may hide an inner structure drastically undermined by unrecognized deterioration. Still, our predisposition is to regard specific episodes of institutional breakdown as exceptions not really reflecting on the institution itself.

It's this same kind of reasoning that often leads people to tolerate dehumanizing or lethargic and wasteful institutional practices—even when they themselves are the victims of those practices. Often they seem to believe that abuse is a necessary, indeed an inevitable, accompaniment of "the system." It's as though to challenge the institution would be just too much to bear. And so we tolerate and rationalize and defend. ("It's not the world's best, but it's the best we've got.")

That kind of thinking in corporations has always led to inaction and resistance to change. "You can't fight the system," says the conventional wisdom. And, as the institutional abuses continue, the conventional wisdom becomes self-fulfilling.

The second premise of this book is prescriptive. It says that corporate organizations must change if they are to survive the changing attitudes and values of the American people. To put it in loftier terms, they must find a soul. Instead of the blind and single-minded pursuit of profit and growth and other narcissistic concerns, corporations must finally turn outward. They must open their eyes to the needs of the people they employ, to the needs of their customers, to the protection of whatever interests their shareholders have, and to the larger interests of the society of which they are a part. All of these needs must be carefully balanced for the good of the organization as well as the whole society.

And right there, of course, is a problem of major proportions because most companies—in practice, if not in pronouncement—have ignored any larger responsibility and pursued their own goals without regard for other concerns. In recent years it has become fashionable for corporations to protest that they are indeed socially aware and socially oriented. Yet in many cases their day-to-day actions mock that claim.

It's a truism that American society is too complex and too interdependent today for any large and powerful corporate organization to dispense with its larger responsibilities to the society. Instead, that organization must strive for a new formulation of its societal role, a role which may be quite different from the one it has played so far.

The third premise of my thesis is the obvious observation that all of this will not happen magically, that there will have to be agents of change. As we look around us, there are many places these agents, these catalysts, could come from. One potential source is the antibusiness interests in our country. Surely they would welcome the chance to deal with the abuses they've been citing. But they might well drive the pendulum too far in the opposite direction and destroy rather than reform the business organization.

Another possible change agent is government. But that's not very promising either, because government traditionally has not understood corporate problems or has offered simplistic solutions or outright (and undiscriminating) condemnation.

The most logical people to help transform business organizations are not its antagonists but the corporate citizens themselves—those people, *at all levels of the organization,* who have the greatest stake in the organization. If the corporation is to succeed in its search for a soul, it will succeed only through the efforts of the corporate body itself. Its redemption must be self-redemption.

The real trouble with most corporations is that their people stand around wringing their hands in anguish and demanding to know when "they" will change things. One of the more important assumptions of this book is that "they" never will. You will. And I will. And we together will. But "they"? Never.

So to sum up my three-part thesis:

- Institutional organizations in general, and corporate organizations in particular, have not kept pace with the changing attitudes and values of American society.
- If such organizations are going to survive in our future-shocked society, they will have to transform themselves so they are more in tune with the society at large.
- That transformation will be accomplished only *from within* the organization by persistent men and women equipped with insight, goodwill, and a large tolerance for frustration and temporary setbacks.

The how and why of this thesis constitute the rest of the book.

That Old Corporate Dogma

The corporate dogma, as I like to call it, is simply the terms in which a business is fond of describing itself. It is not necessarily what a corporation is, but instead it is "the reality" it defines for the public at large and for its own employees. Of course, this dogma was not suddenly pronounced one day from a mountaintop. Instead it has evolved in bits and pieces over the years in response to spoken and implied requests for the business organization to articulate itself and its goals.

From the beginning of the Industrial Revolution in the 1800s to the end of World War I, the proprietors

11

and managers of corporations largely had their own way. The important values were survival of the fittest and the mystique of the self-made man. This was the period, of course, when the industrial corporation took root in America. When it was firmly established and reasonably capable of both survival and growth, it changed its public attitude toward the work force and the society of which it was a part. This change was not really voluntary but was mainly in response to government regulation and the growing strength of labor unions, to name two prime forces.

As those two forces eroded the once brutal power of these companies in the late nineteenth and early twentieth centuries, the company approach to employees was largely changed as well. What emerged from all of this in the 1920s and 1930s was a corporate dogma which was packaged and propagandized with great skill.

It was a dogma intended to explain all the inconsistencies and imperfections of the system and to convince everyone connected in any way with the organization that his welfare and destiny were inextricably tied to the welfare and destiny of the organization itself. Most of all, it allowed and encouraged him to accept the authority, wisdom, and paternalism of the organization, almost unquestioningly.

And, of course, that is the purpose of any dogma—to serve as a formula which eliminates the need for the individual to think the problem through for himself. The dogma was refined and orchestrated through the years, but there were four essential precepts that people could use to explain their work and their lives within the organization—an explanation, incidentally, which has always been a crucial human concern, since it answers man's continuing search for meaning and significance.

Since the early corporate organization was and continued to be a top-down operation heavily dependent on management authority and employee obedience, the dogma seems to have been preoccupied with rationalizing and legitimizing that relationship. Frederick Winslow Taylor, the father of time-and-motion studies, early devised an industrial system which emphasized simplified and fragmented work tasks under continuous supervision. The worker's job was to do as he was told and to increase his output.

In fact, Taylor's classic advice to the worker reflects the authoritarianism of his views and his day:

> For success, then, let me give one simple piece of advice beyond all others. Every day, year in and year out, each man should ask himself, over and over again, two questions. First, "What is the name of the man I am now working for?" and having answered this definitely, then, "What does this man want me to do, right now?"

The Four Dogmatic Precepts

Obviously, as the work force became better educated (and, not coincidentally, as labor unions were formed), this approach was not workable. At this point it became necessary to offer the worker a more thorough explanation of *why* he had to do what he was doing. So enter the dogma, whose first principle is:

Organizations are efficient, well managed, and intelligent. This was the first article of faith, and it was basic to everything else. If you are to believe in any sort of authority, you must first accept the notion that it truly knows best and that it is not only competent but also well intentioned. Once this notion was conceived, it was communicated by business with consummate efficiency and thoroughness to all of American society. In the beginning and until recent times, almost everyone believed.

How many times have you heard someone say with a reassuring wink, "Don't worry. They know what they're doing. They wouldn't be there if they didn't"? Most of us are inclined to believe that those in authority are both competent and upright. That sort of trust is essential to making any authority palatable.

The second article of faith dealt with the intentions and motives of authoritarian managements. It stated that *organizations exist for the benefit of their employees, shareholders, and customers.* Their mission would be merely to serve the balanced best interests of those three groups and the public at large. It was important to convince everyone concerned that this was a mere truism.

The goal of this statement obviously was to remind people that there were many interests to be considered and that the prudent manager had to be a good steward. He could not raise wages *this* year, for example, because such a raise would have to be passed on to the customer or would be contrary to the best interests of the shareholders, who were risking their hard-earned money.

The third precept was the belief that *organizations reward dedication, competence, and performance.* And there, of course, was a very practical principle. If the organization was to grow and prosper, it needed loyal people above all else—people prepared to make all the sacrifices essential to organization success, willing to put the job before anything else in their lives, willing to invest their energies, emotions, and even their health, if need be. Such loyalty has always been for sale, and it was imperative to show that the organization was an appreciative buyer.

The last precept of the dogma was that *organizations are dynamic and receptive to change.* This article of faith was very important indeed because it said, "If you're discouraged today, don't worry, because tomorrow will be better. We're changing and we're working on your problem, so take heart." And, of course, this notion was important to reinforce the other three, for without change it would be impossible to manage efficiently, or to meet the needs of all interested parties, or to reward dedication and performance.

Believers and Unbelievers

These four principles were communicated so effectively to both the employees and the public that they did indeed believe. In fact, when an employee was tempted to question management authority or action, he needed only to have his manager remind him of one

15

or more parts of the dogma and he usually relented. It was such a beautifully orchestrated explanation of his life within the organization!

Clearly, *he* was a potential heretic if he didn't believe these things. Clearly, *his* problem was that he was a selfish individual not willing to make the sacrifices necessary for the greater good of the organization. And clearly he would not be promotable if he persisted in his questioning. Since promotion was to be the driving goal of every red-blooded American worker, that implied or stated threat was supposed to be (and usually was) enough to make him back off.

But let's pause and reflect for a moment on the sort of worker who can function within the confines of that dogma. Obviously, he must believe in self-sacrifice and the need to dedicate himself to worthwhile causes. He must be highly responsive to the prospect of material gain and the corresponding demand that he work harder or more efficiently. He must be capable of loyalty and obedience to management people and to the corporation itself; he must have a fairly strong sense of personal obligation to the organization and to his co-workers. And perhaps most of all, he must trust the system and believe in its pronouncements as well as its good intentions.

In point of fact, as we will see later, there are value shifts occurring in our society to produce corporate employees who tend to disbelieve and reject every single one of those prerequisites. One exception might be the desirability of material gain, but even that traditional American value is being questioned by those born since

World War II and reared in affluence. Given the chance to see that dollars and things do not guarantee personal satisfaction, peace, or happiness, many of them have begun to question materialism as a lifelong value. That questioning has led them to an antibusiness bias.

It amuses me particularly when I hear business people say in response to anti-organization sentiment either outside or inside a particular organization that the answer is "to sell business" to the people. Then they usually go on to say that what we need is a public relations campaign to make "them" understand business problems and goals. The trouble is that the people who make such proposals are almost invariably prepared to try to repackage the traditional corporate dogma and bring it out as a brand-new model to a public preconditioned not to believe and not to buy. Pearl-handled buggy whips are still buggy whips.

Holes in the Dogma

Even if the audience had not changed so drastically as it has since the corporate dogma was first pronounced, it would still find some large holes in the dogma, which we should briefly examine before we move on. Perhaps the greatest difficulty with the dogma was that it seemed to postulate an ideal world peopled by rational and practically incorruptible beings. It tended to overlook human greed, human envy, and the human willingness of management and worker alike to undermine the organization if it is to their personal advantage to do so.

But the dogma did work very well for many years in

holding our companies together. And why shouldn't it? It was all true as far as it went; that is, it was only half true. And that became the problem, because most workers have come to interpret half-truths as outright lies.

Take the first precept, that organizations are efficiently run by competent managements. Sure, organizations are generally efficient and well managed. But many work in spite of themselves rather than because of any great managerial brilliance. And others that are extremely efficient and very well managed go broke. So, to say that a company is prosperous and efficient because it is efficient and well managed is to fall victim to circular reasoning. Good management can be an important cause of success, but it is never the *sole* cause, despite what some authoritarian managements would love us to believe.

The second myth had to do with the question of who is served by the organization. That's a very interesting one. The party line said that organizations are merely means to an end—which is certainly true. But it is *the definition of that end* that creates problems. Historically, companies have responded to the profit motive more than to any other single motivator. And there's certainly nothing wrong or illogical about that. In fact, without profit neither shareholders nor employees would stick with the company.

The problem comes when profit and growth become the *sole* motivators. This leads to the acceptance and invocation of the doctrine that the end justifies the means. For years in this country, no one made any particular demands on our companies not to pollute air and water or not to exploit their labor force. Nor did anyone demand or even expect any display of social responsibility. Companies were in business to make money, and people largely accepted that.

The third myth, to be effective, had to be stated in very simplistic terms. The formula was easy. Work hard, give us your best years and your best efforts, and we will recognize and reward you. It was an irresistible bargain because it was so uncomplicated.

The only problem was that it was impossible to deliver to everybody who followed it. Yet, enough people could be winners to make it all plausible and interesting. Sort of like a lottery with lots of prizes. It was a great way to encourage people to cut one another's throats for personal advantage. On balance, however, it had an irresistible ring of truth that made people alternately competitive and fearful. Nice combination if you want to keep them running full speed in pursuit of company goals.

The fourth and last article of the dogma was that all companies are dynamic and welcome change. Here again is a half-truth. In an autocratic company, change is acceptable only when it benefits those in positions of power. Any change which appears threatening to, or in conflict with, the best interests of the hierarchy can easily be stifled or ignored. Of course, the consequences of ignoring change can be fatal, but the person trying to preserve his power is often incredibly shortsighted about such long-term effects of change.

19

In a Corporate Limbo

So, in very simple terms, these are the main articles of faith which have made up our corporate dogma until very recent times. But our companies are now on the threshold of revolutionary change—change which, whether they like it or not, will be thrust upon them by events.

To a greater or lesser extent our corporate managements are now reacting to some of these events. But I submit that few companies have really faced up to the problems of developing a suitable posture for the twenty-first century. Few are engaged in the serious introspection it will take to transform themselves into the kind of institutions they must become to meet the demands of even the near future.

Our companies are very much like the rest of our institutions. The old dogma is being questioned and discredited, but very little is being done to articulate a new view of what the institution is and must become. Currently, we are in a kind of corporate limbo, in a position somewhere between the old and the new. It is a painful and difficult period because most of our major companies continue to move down the same old road with the vague understanding that times are changing and that they must remake themselves so that they are responsive to the new trends and pressures all around them.

But they don't really understand in any comprehensive way what they are up against.

20

The Corporation and the Value Crunch

One of the first questions we must come to grips with is, Exactly where is the business organization lagging behind the rest of society? (It is important to emphasize, incidentally, that this institutional lag is certainly not peculiar to business. Many of these same things apply to educational institutions, religious institutions, and certainly government organizations.)

To understand the problem it is necessary to look first at what has been happening in the society at large and then to determine how these things have affected business organizations. It seems to me that there are certain trends that have become so obvious in American society that they describe both our condition and our emerging values. I propose to try to identify a half-dozen or so and to suggest what they may portend for the business corporation.

People Count—Things Don't

One clearly emerging new value in our society could be characterized very roughly as "people, not things." It is a reaffirmation of the primacy of human values over doctrines or things. It is also a reaction to some truly monumental social changes in the last 50 years. The small town has virtually disappeared as a self-contained and isolated entity. The church has declined as the focal point of people's social and even spiritual lives. The home has been challenged by all sorts of competing

21

forces and attractions which render it often merely a place of residence. As these things have happened, the individual has lost much of the familiar traditions, support, and love which formerly defined his unique identity. Where his life was once tightly bound by his family, his church, and his community, these boundaries are now far less visible or important.

In bygone days the individual was expected to be loyal to his family, church, and country and to sacrifice his own interests and personal wishes for them. Today he has much greater autonomy of thought and action, and while this liberation from sometimes oppressive pressures and standards is usually welcomed, it does impose demands for personal responsibility which many people aren't equipped to deal with. And certainly this autonomy has tended to rob the individual of some powerful clues which once told him who he was and what was or should be important to him.

Add to those losses the increasing size, complexity, and, therefore, impersonality of the organizations which all of us must relate to in our highly organized contemporary society and it becomes clear that the individual must feel more and more frightened, more and more alone, more and more insignificant.

Then stir into this stew of potential and real assaults on the individual the necessity to somehow keep track of everyone and to devise control systems and information systems. This necessity has led to computerization of practically everything and to the assigning of endless numbers to people—a number for a driver's license, a number to cash one's checks at the supermarket, and on and on until people begin to feel not like whole persons but numbered functions to be monitored and policed.

It's no wonder that people are distressed about this effort to classify and categorize them and to reduce their individual identities to a series of numbers on a punched card. For anyone who thinks and feels at all, this fate is just too threatening, and so he or she naturally fights it in small or large ways. The natural human response is to resist such efforts to depersonalize our lives and to seek whatever ways we can to assert our individual identities.

This resistance may be slight enough to be expressed in the way a person dresses. Or it may go so far that the person opts for an alternative life-style or a second career. Or it may be asserted in any one of the dozens of ways we say to the world: "Look, I'm a person. I'm different. I'm unique. Don't force me to be what I don't want to be."

Whatever else it is, it's an assertion of selfhood, and we all see more and more of it than we used to. In its more extreme form it is the conviction that one's personal fate is more important than any principle or ideal. Self-sacrifice was a value which was admired and held up to young people for generations in Western society. Countless movies were made and books written about the tough hero willing to give his life for a cause, to sacrifice his existence for a higher principle or goal.

In today's less romantic society there seems to be little inclination for the individual to do such things.

Perhaps the most dramatic evidence in recent history was the refusal of many young men to serve in Vietnam, the large number of deserters, and even the refusal of combat platoons in Vietnam to advance under what they regarded as overly hazardous conditions.

Clearly self-sacrifice is not much in vogue today. Perhaps one major reason is that it's difficult, if not impossible, to relate to impersonal organizations in which one is a mere number rather than a valued member. People simply do not sacrifice themselves for causes they don't believe in.

Instant Gratification

A second underlying trend which is relevant to our analysis is the demand for instant gratification and for a high degree of self-indulgence. Largely because of our standard of living and the availability of things, most Americans are able to satisfy a large number of their material wants.

The availability of easy credit, which has turned us into a nation of "ten dollars down and ten dollars a month," has also made it relatively easy for us to acquire many of the things we want. Couple that with relatively high employment and intense advertising that preaches "You owe it to yourself to get it NOW; why wait when you can be the first on the block to own one?" and there is a fairly obvious reversal of the once-traditional American regard for thrift—particularly among young people who have little or no recollection of pre-affluent American society.

Continuing shortages of oil and other necessaries of a high material standard of living, as well as rising unemployment, may reverse some of that in the long run, but for now instant gratification remains a significant American habit.

Future Shock

A third broad trend affecting the corporation is the fantastic rate of change which characterizes modern society. Alvin Toffler has cataloged our reaction to change and has labeled as "future shock" the blunting or outraging of the senses that too much change, too fast, brings to us. But for better or worse, most of us try to swing with change as best we can, believing either that "that's progress" or that we simply have no choice.

One of the by-products of this onrush of change seems to be a lessening of personal loyalty. As older institutions crumble and are not replaced because change overtakes them faster than they can adapt, many people question the logic of consistent and principled behavior and of loyalty to institutions of any type. In a restless and mobile society which discourages "roots," it has become difficult, if not impossible, to build lasting loyalties.

The extreme consequence is that the individual soon can rationalize having no obligations, no loyalties to anyone but himself and perhaps his family and a few close friends. The older loyalties to church, family, hometown, and other institutions of one type or another give way basically to "every man for himself." If you observe people carefully—particularly in large urban areas—there seems to be a noticeable strain on their faces as they move from one stressful situation to another, knowing full well if trouble comes in almost any form, they will probably have to face it alone.

Toffler defends the resolve of so many not to involve themselves in the lives of others as a logical and necessary response to too much change and to the passing through one's life of too many people.[1] But isn't that refusal to involve oneself really the beginning of the breakdown of any organized society? It's a question well worth pondering.

Antisystem Bias

A fourth observable and significant value change in American society is the tendency toward antisystem behavior and attitudes. That probably is a perfectly logical extension of the permissiveness which tends to pervade American families and schools and which has been with us now for close to two generations. It is obviously difficult for a child reared in a permissive environment suddenly to tune himself in to rules and regulations and a highly structured system. He will rebel against it, rail against it, and even sulk openly at its indifference to *his* needs.

He normally is not the person who has much stomach for reforming the system. What he wants is to do away with it altogether, to drop out of it, and to find an unstructured life with no system. The hippie movement of a few years ago was an extreme manifestation of this kind of behavior. That sort of thinking has clearly fed whatever antisystem thinking already existed so that today there seems to be a detectable antisystem bias in our society. Unquestionably that has been fed by Watergate and similar disclosures of organizational abuse.

In May of 1973, a Gallup poll showed that Americans had lost faith in all but two of their institutions during the preceding five years. The two exceptions were organized religion and the public schools, with 66 percent and 58 percent respectively of those polled expressing "a great deal of confidence." At the bottom of the list was big business, with only 26 percent giving their vote of confidence.

The Bullshit Syndrome

Which leads us to the final value change we should consider at this point. There is abroad a feeling which pollster Daniel Yankelovich bluntly describes as the "bullshit syndrome." [2] It is the credibility gap at its worst, the kind of distrust which leads people to respond to some message not with "Is that so?" but with "Bullshit!"

The hostility and distrust reflected by that one word are enough to destroy any specific communication attempt and even to undermine the communication process generally. There is no way to communicate with someone who feels that way about both you and your message.

A Summary

We could go on further identifying such value changes, but for our purposes these are the major ones now affecting the fate of the American corporation. Just how, we'll see shortly. But first let's summarize these emerging trends:

- People are more important than things or abstract principles.
- And yet things are available and desirable, and we all should share in whatever instant gratification we can manage.
- Change is the one constant in life, so let's be pragmatic about everything from morals to personal convictions. There are few, if any, eternal truths. Let's not be obligated to anyone but ourselves.
- The system is a nuisance, an unreasonable restriction on our personal freedom to do as we wish. At best, we will tolerate it and subvert it for our own ends.
- Institutional messages in general, and those from big business in particular, cannot be believed.

How widespread these attitudes really are is obviously open to some conjecture and debate, but there is considerable evidence all around us that they are held by a sizable number of Americans in the 1970s. I have no doubt that even now those attitudes are affecting the American corporation and creating the institutional lag I alluded to earlier. I believe that people are measuring their experience and their lives inside the organization against the values they have acquired outside the organization, and—though I can't prove it with any firm data—that they are using those values as a grindstone to reshape and smooth the old corporate dogma.

In the next chapter let's go inside the corporation and look out at the rest of the world.

CHAPTER II

A View
from the Inside Out

Corporate Myths versus Corporate Realities

CRITICS of business sometimes suggest that there are
dark conspiracies being hatched all through the business
community to victimize the unwary public. This has
always been an easy fear to prey on. There is a streak
of paranoia in all of us, and when actual conspiracies—
no matter how small or clumsy—are exposed, someone
invariably shouts a triumphant "I told you so" and
launches an investigation to expose the whole industry,
or the whole party, or the whole government, or the
whole something.

It seems that we would prefer to believe in well-
organized and clever plotters than in an indifferent and

amoral system. Ergo, when things go wrong, we assume that the conspirators have struck again to cause a shortage, silence a critic, or even assassinate a president or political leader. What I mean, of course, is not that powerful men never scheme against the public interest, but simply that they are not nearly so well-organized, so shrewd, so ruthless, so effective, and so numerous as we are sometimes led, or want, to believe.

The Nature of Corporate Power

With that as a preface, let's look briefly at the business corporation as an influential force in modern society, even as a possible premeditating and malicious conspirator against the public good. There is no question that corporations individually and collectively control vast amounts of wealth and have at their disposal the means to determine what is available for us to consume, to urge us to buy whatever they have produced and are selling, and to command the talents and to some extent the destinies of large numbers of us. In some instances they can even influence domestic or foreign governmental policy by virtue of their holdings, their power, and their connections.

To most of us, if we bother to think about it, that kind of power is both imposing and intimidating. In fact, however, that power is more potential than real. The good news and the bad news are that our corporations are bureaucracies which are not operated at the wave of a hand by cigar-chomping, button-pushing autocrats. Like all bureaucratic organizations they oper-

31

ate on consensus and on a careful balancing of one set of interests against another. And like all bureaucracies, they are more or less beset with inertia, inefficiency, and caution.

Further, those who argue that the large corporation represents a substantial threat to the public interest have overlooked the real nature of corporate power and of the corporate bureaucrat, who more than anything else is dedicated to the preservation of the system which sustains him. My point is that if corporations get into trouble with the public today, it is not a premeditated plot of some sort that gets them there. It is usually a case of their behaving according to the ground rules and values of the system and then discovering that—for various reasons they don't comprehend or agree with— someone outside the system has either challenged or changed the rules.

Private Profits versus Public Priorities

With respect to slippery ground rules, the oil shortage of 1974 provides a perfect case in point. Daily there were newspaper accounts of public officials and private citizens who charged the oil companies with price fixing, profit gouging, and conspiracy. In one Associated Press story an oil company spokesman moaned, "The oil we're talking about is in fields that are in secondary and tertiary recovery stages. . . . It's very expensive to produce. . . . To some people, I know that's going to sound evil. But we have a business proposition here. It's hardheaded business economics." To which a government official responded with the public view: "It may make good business sense to leave that oil in the ground. But is it right to place that high a priority on profits in the midst of an energy crisis?" [1]

At congressional hearings on the subject, the top executives of the major oil companies explained in clear and unmistakable market terms why they had run their businesses the way they had. Quite simply, they had tried to keep their risks and overhead at a level consistent with strong profit performance and the long-term best interests of their organizations. They had even issued warnings that an energy shortage could easily develop if their particular market system were not given government support and relief in the form of tax incentives and higher prices.

No wonder that the oil executives were upset by public criticism. In their view, they had done only what they were paid so handsomely to do. Now, however, someone was changing the ground rules and making the change retroactive, so that their past practices could be condemned. The public interest was going to be held up to them as a much greater concern than corporate profits and growth.

In this whole episode we have an instructive morality play for all contemporary businessmen. First, consistent with the shifting values cited earlier, people *are* being regarded as more important than things (including large oil companies and their profit structure), and second, institutional messages and motives alike are suspect. Continued failure to understand these two points could conceivably lead to the nationalization of the oil industry.

The Decision-Making Process

I believe it's safe to say from the evidence presented to date that conspiracy is not the problem. An unhealthy insensitivity to public needs and problems is probably more like it. Normally such corporate insensitivity is a product of the single-mindedness which motivates most of our companies. To develop a better understanding of that, let's take a look at the decision-making process in a corporation.

The senior executives are normally in the position of choosing among a number of alternatives presented to them by their subordinates with recommendations for action. The task of these decision-makers is to balance all their concerns about profit, growth, and the uncertainties of the future and to make a choice. That is their primary organization role, and for the company to carry on successfully they had better be good choosers. Rarely, if ever, do they do the spade work. Rarely are they close to all the primary sources. Instead they identify problems, pose questions, and put people to work to find solutions. What comes back to them in reports, computer printouts, and sometimes dazzling audiovisual presentations is the consensus of the ostensibly talented people they employ.

The astute executive is the person who can poke and probe at what is being offered and expose the fallacies, the risks, and the distortions no matter how slick the report or presentation. It is an art that is not readily learned but that generally goes along with an incisive and somewhat skeptical mind.

The decision-maker in the typical large organization generally lacks first-hand knowledge of a problem. Of necessity, he must experience things vicariously through the people who work for him. There isn't time for any other approach, because of the size and complexity of the problems he deals with. In effect, then, he is at the mercy of the talents and thoroughness of his subordinates. This dependence makes him uncomfortable, and it also on occasion leads him to some bad decisions.

John Kenneth Galbraith calls this kind of corporate decision-making "collegial"; that is, a number of specialists share in recommending the decision which is nominally made by one man. He says this is typical in large organizations.[2] Galbraith is right, and the popular conception of the corporate autocrat forcing his decision on everyone else is dead wrong.

There are a number of problems inherent in the collegial technique. One of these very often is the cowardice of the specialists or the decision-maker or both. Those recommending a given decision may very well recommend what they think the boss wants to hear. Or the boss may be so intimidated by what he sees as the group will that he okays what he really thinks is only a marginally valuable idea.

Another problem is the single-mindedness that often motivates such decision-making. There is a good deal of inertia in any organization, and once the corporate ship is on any given course, it takes a mighty pull on the wheel to change direction. And even then the change in course is often painfully slow. Some critics see in this the fatal flaw in the bureaucratic corporation's attempts to cope with today's rate of change. Obviously that remains to be seen.

Profits Come First

Perhaps the best example of the large corporation's single-mindedness is the typical concentration on profit and growth to the exclusion or subordination of practically everything else. Some observers claim that this is the discipline that keeps the organization together, that prevents it from pursuing frivolous and irrelevant goals. Some even assert that without this single-mindedness, such organizations would simply collapse.

Nobody in his right mind questions the need for profits. But if that need becomes such an intense pressure that it distorts other interests, priorities, and goals of the organization, adversely affects the public interest, and leads management to unethical, immoral, or irresponsible behavior then it clearly is out of hand.

In propagating the corporate dogma, business leaders often made the case that we were all in this thing together, that there was no conflict between the needs of the employee, the needs of the shareholder, and the needs of the customer. In fact, it was widely proclaimed that serving the customer's and the shareholder's interests would make the business more profitable, and that the ensuing increase in income would benefit the employee through more job opportunities and better salaries. All of which was plausible, except that it begged the question of what happens in a crunch.

Because of the need to keep revenues and profits above certain specified levels and to hold overhead below certain levels, the we're-in-this-thing-together premise breaks down in practice. In any profit squeeze, corporate managements seek relief by reducing overhead, and that, unfortunately, often means laying off employees.

You could easily deplore that action unless you understand that those are the stipulated rules that corporate managements must live by. Maximum profit balanced against the short- and long-term welfare of the corporation is the name of the game, and it is the yardstick by which the performance of senior managers is measured.

The Pursuit of Survival

Besides the need to meet certain profit goals, the corporate planners have traditionally set their sights on the following list of what we might call "survival priorities":

- The pursuit of a salable product that could win a "reasonable" share of the available market.
- The pursuit of planned, orderly, and maximum growth.
- Increased worker productivity and decreased operating costs.
- The ability to raise capital through the sale of stock and/or borrowing.

37

These priorities have pretty much shaped specific actions and the behavior of business corporations. They have also led to more than a few abuses and have even persuaded some managements to produce and promote products with little utility or social value. Not a few critics have contrasted the surplus of brands of body deodorants and of fast-food hamburger franchises and the multitude of brands of cigarettes and other items of questionable worth with the scarcity of adequate and inexpensive housing or suitable medical care. It would certainly be irrational to blame McDonald's for a shortage of adequate housing, but the pressure of the profit motive has not always led us to deal with the most serious needs of our society first. Sometimes, in fact, it has done just the opposite.

The Threat of Cynicism

At this point it would be well to pause and see where this whole line of reasoning has been taking us. First, the conspiratorial view of business and business strategy is about as logical as most conspiracy theories are in explaining human behavior. For one thing, it makes humans out to be much cleverer and more sinister than they are. People managing a large business just don't have the enormous amount of time or energy that it takes to conspire (except possibly against one another, but that's a separate subject we'll examine later).

Further, power in corporate organizations is widely diffused. Rarely does any one person have enough of it to act on his own. Instead he must seek and act on consensus. And the realities of taking responsibility in large organizations are such that he usually wants to seek counsel and to share the decision and the responsibility with his counselors. Sharing power to that extent also tends to make conspiracy a risky business.

In general, the responsibility in a corporate organization is on one person's shoulders so there can later be a symbolic hero (victim) if one is needed. But decisions are mostly collegial when they are being worked out.

The root of the corporate problem and the explanation of most corporate behavior, then, is the matter of what really motivates corporate management and decision-making. As we have seen, the traditional and primary motivators are the need for profit and the institution's survival, the need for increasing worker productivity and reducing any cost which reduces profit, and the need to raise capital.

Viewed objectively in those terms, the business corporation has little time or energy to deal with—except as secondary concerns—the human needs of the consumer. And those limitations apply also to the larger and perhaps even contradictory needs (i.e., the need for clean air versus the economic need to retain x number of heavy-manufacturing jobs) of the community in which the corporation operates and whose natural resources it must use either as raw materials or as the repository for its waste products. In practice, the primary concerns of survival, growth, and self-perpetuation become so compelling and so threatening to management that the "secondary" concerns are either ignored or given lip service.

The trouble is that the corporate dogma never tells us that. In fact, it leads us to believe that all of the primary and secondary concerns are balanced and equal. And we spend an inordinate amount of time and energy trying to square our real experiences with corporations with the fiction of the dogma. For most people it's a bewildering, if not a maddening, experience that leaves them wondering whom or what to believe. The resulting discrepancy between the way it is and the way it is supposed to be tends to make cynics of the very people who can and must be the agents of change and of responsible corporate behavior.

In the final analysis, that cynicism may be the greatest threat of all to our corporate organizations and even to our society at large, for cynicism leads us to disbelieve even in the *possibility* of reform or repair.

When sufficient numbers of people reach that condition, the organization becomes largely incapable of serious self-renewal of either its good intentions or its purpose. And *that* is the grave danger, because today's changing world will require—is already requiring—American corporations to shift some of their priorities. Thinking those shifts through is difficult and delicate work which can be done only by people who understand what is happening and who appreciate and are committed to the welfare of the corporation and of human beings everywhere.

At the least, that work will take men and women

with a vision. Such people never have been plentiful, but today they are particularly scarce. More on that subject later on. For now let us simply mark it as a point to come back to and to analyze further.

Some Other Trends

There are two other current corporate trends which also should be noted because they muddy the waters even further. One is the growing multinational character of many of our corporations. The other is the machinations of finance capitalists and conglomerate managers, who have made it difficult for us to understand who "owns" some of our corporations and, therefore, who is responsible for their actions.

I will not attempt to address either of those complex trends in the limited space of this book except to note that they are merely among the most important developments now affecting business operating policies, plans, and strategies. I don't believe that anyone yet knows for sure the full implications of these two developments. On the one hand, they are leading to significant changes in both global employment patterns and the distribution of goods and money. On the other, they are leading to increasing concentration of economic power.

For the purposes of this discussion, the unanswered —and perhaps at this point the unanswerable—question is not whether anyone's intentions are good or evil but whether we will create an international financial and economic system which is so large and so complex that no one will really understand how it operates or how to manage it.

But that, at best, is a moot point. What we do know is that the world's resources are finite. What we also know is that in the face of continuing shortages of food and energy, we must re-examine our long-held faith that any sort of growth is, by definition, good, that growth and progress are synonymous.

Writing in *The Wall Street Journal* in 1972, David Anderson raised a question that surely will be the subject of debate and discussion for years to come. In fact it may well be the most important issue we grapple with in the third century of our republic. He said:

> . . . for centuries men have lived in societies where national and personal development have not been intense, life-molding goals. They have remained "underdeveloped" though those who believe comforts of the spirit are as important as material comforts can question whether such societies are worse off than our own, all things considered. The job for America, in the end, may be to replace the idea of success with the idea of the soul.[3]

How Does It Feel to Work in a Big Corporation?

Your subjective view of life is an important consideration in any large organization, whether it be business, governmental, military, or educational. That view will depend on a number of things: Where in the hierarchy do you sit? How much control do you have over your job tasks, day-to-day working decisions, security of employment, rate of compensation, work hours, freedom to come and go without close supervision? And on and on. It's all very iffy, but there are some common measures we can examine to tell us how a job feels.

Are Our Basic Needs Satisfied?

The behavioral scientists say it in a variety of ways, but most of them agree that there are certain basic needs which any job must satisfy. In general every employed person requires the fulfillment of two basic needs merely to survive.

The first is job *mastery*. The employee must master some kind of job skill to the point where he can perform it routinely to his employer's satisfaction. That's the basic matter of job competence.

The second requirement is *predictability*. Most of us must be reasonably confident that action X in the organization is likely to result in reaction Y. If the elements of the job are constantly changing and producing continually changing reactions from the organization, we tend to become tense and bewildered, like the child raised by inconsistent parents.

If the levels of job mastery and predictability are consistent with our individual needs, some other higher-level responses are often called for. It is usually at this point that we crave *recognition* for our efforts. We want to feel valued as worthy members of the organization and as unique contributors and individuals.

And if that need should be satisfied, then we are

43

ready to reciprocate, to give something back to the organization, and *to participate* as members in good standing. The management experts say all of this in different ways, but these four human needs are a part, in one way or another, of all of their descriptions of how people react to organizations and to work.

In point of fact, most organizations are not very good at dealing with these human needs. In their early and formative years, when things are less systematized and when there is usually rapid growth and expansion, they seem to do a better job in providing exciting and challenging jobs.

But there seems to be an almost inexorable aging process that robs organizations of their vitality and of their ability to satisfy human needs. The in-group becomes more concerned with preserving and increasing its power. Challenge and dissent are discouraged, ignored, or punished. The familiar and traditional are preserved even if they are no longer suitable due to changing circumstances. And, in time, the members of the organization begin to believe that there is no use in innovating. The vision that energized the organization in the first place fades and is lost.

All of us have seen enough of these kinds of organizations to know how they feel, and how they feel is usually pretty miserable. The trouble is that organizations tend to become so entrenched and so ossified that they literally take on an existence of their own, an existence which can become so real and so tangible that it overpowers the will and even the rights of the members. In time the organization itself becomes the greater good whose well-being and survival dominate every decision, every action. Dr. Margaret Hennig of Simmons College put it about as bluntly as it can be put:

> Corporate life leaves much to be desired. Take a look at what really makes most corporations operate at the top and tell me it isn't political. . . . Take a look at what the American corporation in general demands of the man. It asks him to place his allegiances with the company before himself or his family or anyone else. Sometimes very subtly, but it asks it. It asks him to be willing to place at the top of his priority list his job before anything else. It asks him to respond to any demand that it makes of him, at any time, under any conditions. And in return, it tells him very little about what he does well and a great deal about what he doesn't do well. . . . It says to him, "Buddy, when you come through the door in the morning, this place does not allow emotional life." . . . It asks that you live 2000—and for an executive, 4000—hours a year in a climate and in an environment in which the basic affections of human beings are primarily taboo. It is a climate in which love is not allowed. It is a climate in which kindness is devalued. It is a climate in which concern for people is called "soft." . . . Okay it has its rewards—money, status, position, recognition—all the things we have promulgated here as important. All external things, all controlled by others and where are we [women] and where is man? [4]

The Changing Success Ethic, a 1973 Survey Report by the American Management Associations, tends to confirm Dr. Hennig's views of life in the corporation. Among the approximately 3000 American businessmen who responded to the survey, 40 percent of all middle managers and 52 percent of all supervisory managers described their work as unsatisfying. The survey tended to blame their lack of satisfaction on one or more of the following problems:

- 16 percent claimed their companies did not give them sufficient opportunity to realize their career goals.
- Better than 50 percent said there was too much pressure to conform to company standards.
- Nearly 30 percent said the job had adversely affected their health in the last five years.
- The majority claimed that progress on the job depended on the following factors: (1) their ability and willingness to please their immediate boss, (2) a dynamic personality, and (3) "who you know." [5]

In general they tended to ignore or reject the traditional success formula of competence, hard work, and accomplishment. No matter what the dogma said, their experience as they perceived it in the real day-to-day world of business was telling them something else.

Causes of Dissatisfaction

Perhaps in looking at this subjective issue of how it feels to be part of a large organization, the more important question is, If the organization is like this, why is it? What is there in the situation—and perhaps even inherent in it—that makes large numbers of managers (and others) claim they are dissatisfied and unfulfilled?

It seems to me that there are four basic causes of managerial dissatisfaction. Each is a far-ranging and complex subject in itself, but we must understand all these phenomena before we can really understand contemporary corporate alienation.

The first basic cause is the almost obsessive desire of people in almost any kind of hierarchical organization (and that includes practically all organizations) to move up the organization to what they see as positions of power.

The second is related to the first. It is the existence of office politics and the bare-knuckle and bared-fang kind of assault it often leads to for the sake of personal advantage.

The third cause is our peculiar naiveté about work and our assumption that it will fulfill all of our material, personal, and even spiritual needs.

And the fourth is the simple fact that work is becoming less *real* for large numbers of the population, the so-called knowledge workers in particular, who do not make any tangible product but merely contribute their knowledge to a process or a system. In a sense they are like blindfolded assembly-line workers who have the sensory experience of feeling and manipulating parts of a process or product but are never able to see any tangible or lasting outcome of their efforts. Let's examine each one of these causes briefly.

The Urge to Move Up. The American value of getting ahead is so deeply ingrained that most of us have embraced it unthinkingly and practically without reservation. In fact, to question it (until very recently) was to be guilty of a modern heresy. Even today, when more people are beginning to question the mindless pursuit of material possessions, there are few people who are

47

able to resist the carrot of more and more status, more and more power.

It is close to an article of faith that one enters an organization at a given step and then casts an eye to the top and impatiently climbs onward and upward to more and more responsibility and greater rewards. The entire system is designed to encourage that kind of behavior. Indeed, when the system detects the occasional person who is genuinely uninterested in climbing the hierarchy or who opts to quit climbing at some comfortable plateau, it does not know what to make of such behavior. Until very recently such a person has generally had to expend great amounts of time and energy faking intense concentration on the top and feeling slightly guilty about his lack of drive and ambition.

But in truth, most people have joined the race with little outside urging. They have been only too willing to run the corporate maze, scurrying from alley to alley in search of the path to their reward—or their punishment. Obviously, when anyone makes himself or herself a victim of such external judgment and reward, he or she has largely surrendered the ability for self-evaluation and even self-esteem. One's worth in such a situation is a precarious product of other people's opinions and other people's standards. For most of us this is a painful dependency which tends, consciously or unconsciously, to grate on us and to heighten our sense of separation from our inner selves.

If we don't remain in motion toward the top (and obviously most of us will not), we often experience a sense of failure and incompleteness. And ironically even when we *are* achieving rather substantial results, we can still be victimized by that persistent inner voice which says, "It's not enough. Keep going."

Office Politics and Office Warfare. Closely related to this drive for more and more success, more and more power, is the bitter reality of office politics. No one who has ever been ambushed at the water cooler or knifed at a conference table by either an adversary or a friend can easily forget the experience. The assault is often unpremeditated, but the obsession to move ahead tends to blunt one's conscience and one's sense of right and wrong.

In my 15 years in business I have been amazed at people's capacity to crawl over and around the corpses of co-workers, subordinates, and superiors on their way to the next foothold on the corporate pyramid. It is not merely the competitive spirit as much as it is an instinct for the jugular, an instinct that has usually been fed by successful past battles. That does not mean that all, or most, people who make it to the top do so by means of their willingness to do the competition in. In fact, I still believe, though I could never prove it, that the truly ruthless eventually get theirs and that the ones who actually rise to the very top do so *mainly* because of their competence. At those rarefied levels you have to have more than guile and cunning to hang on.

Mostly it's the middle of organizations that is the no-man's-land of corporate combat. And it's the struggle for position and power there that is the most ruthless and the most costly in our large organizations. Since most of us are destined to spend our working careers in the trenches, the day-to-day work life of a corporate employee is likely to be more combative than he or she would choose, if choice were possible.

Much of that is a product of simple job insecurity. Management psychologist Robert N. McMurry told the *National Observer* in an interview on the subject:

> I'd say 75 percent of corporation employees, including a lot of presidents and vice presidents, are very anxious, fearful people by nature, fundamentally insecure. Much of the internal conflict that takes place grows out of people's reactions to what they perceive as threats to their security. . . . I can't tell you the number of companies I've seen composed of cringing wretches.[6]

McMurry has put his finger on the cause of what some of my friends and associates in business refer to as the "CYA syndrome." "CYA" is shorthand for "cover your ass." It is the elaborate explanation or excuse usually presented in writing and circulated in anticipation of or in the wake of a disaster. It absolves the writer of all blame and fairly often suggests or tells where and on whom the real blame should be put.

In most cases it is a sniveling and contemptible document written by someone in mortal terror of losing his position on the ladder. It is not the kind of corporate footrace which most of us expect and are willing to take our chances with if we have any confidence in our skills. Instead, it is a kick to the groin, a swift elbow blow, or a shove administered without warning, usually by someone we are expected to work closely with and to trust. A sorry state of affairs—but typical of the ruthlessness which can be seen in almost any organization from the church to ITT on any given business day.

The Search for Fulfillment. Perhaps the thing which collectively makes us such sitting ducks for the office bully or assassin is our unrealistic expectations of what a job can do for us. We have been led to believe (mainly by television portrayals, advertising, and the movies, to cite only a few such major influences in our culture) that life's real pleasures are to be found in a career. Playing and winning the game of work are what it's all about. You are whatever your work identity is. So one person *is* a doctor, another *is* a teacher, a third *is* a business executive, and on and on. This identity becomes very important to its owner as a means of flashing instant credentials to the world. It is useful at cocktail parties, in neighborhood chats, and, sadly, even in impressing one's friends and family.

As an aside, it seems to me that the women's movement is developing almost an obsession with work as identity. The role of housewife and mother is being devalued or acknowledged only in patronizing terms as fit for a half-wit, while practically any sort of salaried career is held up as true fulfillment. I fear the movement is about to stub its toe badly on this issue as the inevitable frustrations of organization life make themselves felt.

The point for both men and women is that this identification of self with work tends to make one's job progress *the* central fact of his or her existence and to turn the job into a grim win-or-lose proposition played

51

with an intensity reserved for very few of life's other activities. Hence the obsession with movement. Hence the obsession with office politics and the power struggle.

In a sense it's even worse for the non-career-oriented worker and for blue collar workers. The signals from the rest of society tell them that they're nonparticipants in the only game in town that counts. So they must be content with other satisfactions, other means of fulfillment.

Separation from End Products. Obviously, as automation and computerization change the nature of work, and as more and more people leave the assembly line for the role of knowledge worker or for the task of button-pusher as opposed to "doer," the sense of separation from the work we do will become more acute.

In the typical office or professional job it is very difficult to identify one's efforts with any tangible and lasting product. Recommendations, reports, memos, and the like are not a satisfactory end product. Nor is there much sense of participation in sitting at a computer console which monitors the performance of an automatic assembly line. Our inability to touch, push, or tug at present-day work can only deepen the sense of separation imposed on us by large, impersonal organizations.

So here we sit, sharing a vessel and a voyage which was originally billed as a pleasure cruise but which has afflicted a great many of us with an ill-defined motion sickness. Before we examine any of the possible means we might have at our disposal to deal with both the symptoms and the sickness itself, let's look at one of the major causes of corporate angst. It is the cause I have been implying so far without actually stating it: Our maps of the territory are mostly wrong. We'll see how in the next section.

You've Got to Know the Territory

The old drummer's slogan that "You gotta know the territory" certainly applies to corporate life, as it does to a good many other things. But the trouble is that the maps most people have been given of the corporation don't match the terrain. Corporate life is not a mere mixture of hard work, dedication, clear and rigid organization charts, crisp plans, efficiency, and the survival of the fittest, despite what most of the maps imply. It is partly those things, but they ignore at least two of the ever present realities of the corporation—the roles of power and leadership.

Those two subjects, when they are ever discussed, are usually couched in all sorts of platitudes about management and management practice. But the subject of power per se is rarely, if ever, mentioned. I suppose there are two reasons. One is that the word "power" is so abstract that it is difficult to comprehend except in rather vague and unsettling terms. The other is that it is a subject which frightens most of us because either we look at ourselves as being the victim of someone else's power (and therefore feel helpless and anxious about our ability to control our own fate) or we see ourselves as holding power over others and are troubled by the responsibility or even the ability to determine another's fate.

The result of these two concerns is the same. We simply pretend that power is not a factor within our organizations, or we look on it as the concern of diabolical personalities determined to take away our freedom to act in our own behalf. In either case we view the whole thing as a kind of organizational obscenity not to be discussed openly or given much thought.

The other poorly understood organizational reality, which is closely related to power, is leadership. We talk much more openly about this subject, but we have seen fit to define it in all kinds of theories about how managers manage. The result is a mishmash of ideas which are perceived as polar (autocratic versus participative) and which confuse the aspiring manager because they seem to offer him how-to systems which are mutually exclusive and which appear to be offered as rival prescriptions for success.

A treatise on these two subjects is certainly worth at least a book in itself, so I will limit myself to a few observations gleaned from my own organization experience.

What Is Power?

Power and leadership are slippery subjects, but it's important to recognize their existence in the organization. Otherwise you too will likely use the wrong maps. Very simply, power is the ability of a person or a system to control or influence the behavior of others in an organization. It is held by corporate presidents. It is held even more obviously and directly by first-line supervisors.

In most organizations, as I noted earlier, power is so widely shared that very few individuals really possess very much of it; and yet power held over us individually can seem almost absolute. Perhaps one of the truisms of corporate life is that most of us spend a fair amount of our time trying to subvert others' power over us. In our culture, at least, individual freedom is a highly prized possession, so early in life we learn to poke and prod at the system to see what it will or won't allow. We become experts in the art of the possible and in the art of keeping the leash around our necks just as loose as we can without causing it to be jerked back sharply and painfully.

And perhaps the intelligent exercise of that ability is the fundamental difference between effectiveness or failure within any organization. There are some who are vaguely offended that anyone should hold power over their destinies. They rail against it, they sulk about it, and they lament the unfairness of it. But their protest is usually based on the fallacy that freedom is the opposite condition from being subject to someone's power. Further, they are under the misapprehension that power is imposed upon them arbitrarily by someone in authority.

The hard fact is that we usually grant power. And we grant it quite freely and willingly to those who really hold power over us—in the sense of their being able to control our behavior. Think of the sort of manipulation we lay ourselves open to when we respect, admire, or love another person. Our willingness to please and to have our feelings reciprocated can lead to all sorts of control over us.

The freest, most independent human among us—if he is truly human and feeling—is easily a victim of this sort of power. So the notion that you can avoid external control over your behavior—a notion which some people today actually and mistakenly try to act out in their lives—is romantic nonsense.

Corporate Power Techniques

The only real question for us as individuals is, To whom will we choose to assign power over our actions and our goals? And in that fact lies a very important insight for the organization. There are two ways in which the organization traditionally has tried to wield power over its members. One is through sheer imposition of authority. The other is by encouraging internal competition for whatever power was available in the organization largely to keep the members from being complacent.

The Authoritarian Approach. Given the negative view toward authority these days, the purely autocratic approach does not look very promising. Even the military seems to be backing off from its customary view that "we take away your rights and give them back to you one at a time as privileges."

In industry this authoritarian view of life is even less promising. For example, one of the continuing work concerns of the United Automobile Workers has been the *quality* of the work environment. Some automotive workers in recent years have even sported large buttons stating, "Don't tell me! Ask me!"

The Internal-Competition Approach. The other, and more insidious, power technique in industry is encouraging internal competition for jobs and for status. The theory behind this is twofold. First, it is believed that this sort of footrace will benefit the organization in bringing to management the most qualified and strongest candidates. Second, it is thought it will tend to prevent complacency and to force people to work harder and more efficiently in their race to personal advantage. The assumption has been that the organization would be the beneficiary in both cases. In practice, however, it is questionable if anybody wins, least of all the organization itself.

For the individual, one of the consequences of no-holds-barred internal competition is to make the corporate internal environment so real and so vivid a part of the job that it becomes a preoccupation. Any corporate employee who is concentrating on the political schemes and machinations of his fellows—and that's usually what that kind of competition means—is usually doing so at the expense of the only environment that really counts for the corporation, namely the external world of the customer where the business makes it or doesn't make it.

Peter Drucker has reminded us that what happens inside a company results in cost; it's what happens *outside* that leads to customer satisfaction and profits. He also has noted that the effective corporate performer tends to look upward for management direction and outward to the marketplace for results rather than downward and inward, which inevitably leads to generation of additional cost rather than profit.[7]

What could be more useless to the corporation than internal competition, which tends to set people against one another and to engender mutual distrust while preoccupying everyone with an activity which has little if any company benefit? You can rest assured that insecure people and warring factions are doing little, if anything, to move the organization toward its goals. They're far too busy with their own goals and with each other.

Another erroneous corporate map is the one which suggests that people can conduct power raids on one another's domain. Power is not an inherent part of a job. It is like the goose's golden eggs. Do in the goose and that's the end of the eggs. Do in the effective performer in hopes of grabbing off what he's got, and you often find that what he had was more a product of his own unique skills and initiative than it was a job description or a box on the organization chart.

And yet there are large numbers of corporate citizens who believe that the power struggle and winning are what corporate life is all about. Perhaps I am naive or have led a sheltered life, or both, but I have yet to see the truly vicious infighter win the fight—over the distance. They're able to win lots of rounds, but eventually their brutality sickens or threatens others—who then somehow band together to rid the organization of its little Caesar.

But worse than this enmity, and one of the saddest

and most destructive results of internal competition and office politics, is their tendency to obscure both good and bad performance. In the long run the best interests of any organization are served by identifying good performers and moving them to the positions where they can make their best contribution. Similarly, poor performance must be identified and dealt with in some intelligent and compassionate fashion.

But any manager preoccupied with his own survival neglects that task. And worse, he often resorts to the shabby tactic of not recognizing—or even stealing credit for—the work of subordinates or co-workers, usually out of his fear of building competitors for his job. At its worst this sort of rivalry is carried on between entire work groups in a company, with one department secretly cheering and rejoicing over the failures of a "competitive" group. In that kind of conflict it is almost impossible to measure individual performance. The mudslinging is too intense and the finger-pointing too common to allow objective evaluation of any one person's performance. Common sense tells us that the organization is the ultimate loser even more than the maligned performer.

The Need for True Leaders

Instead of this shabby business, what is truly required of organization management is leadership—that difficult-to-define and rather rare quality which induces people to *assign* power over themselves to a manager whom they respect and trust. That is probably the only kind of power which is really effective in today's world.

What is the lesson for corporate organizations in all of this? I think it's absolutely clear that more than anything else they should be trying to produce managers who are able to rise above power politics and to engender in their subordinates a feeling of confidence and the belief that they can trust the boss as well as the organization. By no means do I believe that that task is a simple one. In fact, it may be an impossibility. At least so far, no one seems to know how to train or produce that sort of leader.

The magic combination of qualities reads like something out of a knight-errant's chivalric handbook, but I fervently believe that the effective manager managing in the balanced best interests of his company and his people must be intelligent, must be a person with a sustaining vision of what life is and what it can be, must be a person of integrity, and must be passionately dedicated to finding and telling the truth.

If that sounds to you as though I believe that life in the organization is a noble calling for a person motivated by some old-fashioned virtues, you're right. The Greek word *agape* originally was defined as "a love of one's fellow humans that could permit self-sacrifice." As dumb and as unfashionable as that may sound to the corporate cynic, that's what I believe the good manager is called upon to do. And if he has the courage and the inclination to do so, he will be assigned power by his people beyond anything a title or an organization chart could ever give him. That's leadership.

One of my closest friends is an ex-pro tackle, a giant

of a man with a heart and soul to match. For years I tried to persuade him to go to football games with me, but he refused. I was always curious why he had so little interest in watching a sport in which he had been so successful and then one day, with some evident embarrassment, he told me. First his college education and then his livelihood had literally depended on his ability to batter another human being physically. "I just became sick of trying to whip another person and even seeing a few lying injured at my feet and knowing that I was responsible."

Somehow, until he told me how it felt, I never really realized how physical and brutal the game was. The bruises and the pain were invisible to me. The running and the action were all that was visible, and I hadn't had any notion as a spectator what it must feel like for the players.

Maybe in corporations, when enough of us are like my friend and are disgusted with injuring our fellow humans, the carnage will end. Maybe.

In the next section we'll see why the corporate reward system is set up in such a way that it often actually discourages an end to that sort of behavior.

What's Wrong with the Corporate Reward System

In the idealized terms of the corporate dogma, the corporate reward system has always been depicted as a crucial management technique for rewarding that behavior thought to move the corporation toward its goals.

Specifically, it elaborated on the simple claim that organizations reward dedication, competence, and performance, saying that the system was designed to:

- *Identify* those who make the most important contributions to company success.
- *Promote* those who are most capable of leading.
- *Develop* further the skills of those who seem to have the greatest leadership potential.
- *Base* people's compensation on their actual performance on the job.

In reality, the corporate reward system has never been that effective in identifying the good performers and in moving them ahead. As happens so often in organizations, somewhere between stated goals and actual performance, cold Reality rears her not-so-pretty head. According to the corporate skeptics, the reward system in practice has very different qualities from those ascribed to it:

- It rewards those who set their sights on pleasing the boss, period.
- It rewards those with patrons in high places.
- It rewards those with dynamic, outgoing personalities—the best talkers and the charmers.
- It even rewards those who exploit people in the attainment of short-term goals.

Why this discrepancy between stated goals and perceived performance? The obvious reason is that, in the corporate dogma, we describe an idealized reward system which never really existed and which probably is not possible given our seeming inability to measure performance and people with any real accuracy.

On a somewhat analogous issue, lay theologian Michael Novak once wrote, "We Americans *want* to be moral so ardently that we begin to believe that we are a good people. . . . But what if the American heart is not particularly good, but rather like all the other hearts in the world—mediocre and evil, beautiful and avaricious, generous and mean?"

It could also be said that in corporations we want so badly to do the right thing that we assert that the good guys always *do* get their just rewards. Anyone who has done much time at a desk knows that that is simply not true. One of the great deficiencies among line managers is their inability or even unwillingness to judge the performance of their people against objective standards.

And so we face the discouraging truth that despite the appearance of objective and scientific evaluation,

- Managers sometimes promote their favorites and not the best performers.
- Or mediocre performers are given performance ratings and raises similar, if not equal, to those of the best performers.
- Or a manager who chews up the people resource sometimes is recognized as someone who can be counted on "to get the job done."
- Or a manager may permit his experiences and biases to work unfairly against minorities, ethnic groups, women, and other human beings.

There are no easy remedies. Perhaps the *only* remedy is for all of us to acknowledge that the goal of applying an objective reward system in an objective fashion is an ideal worth striving for but probably no more attainable than any other ideal we know about.

The Wrong Kind of Motivation

The trouble is that over the years we have persuaded large numbers of people that pay and promotion are about the only job measures that matter. And we have encouraged a scramble for these as the only rewards that look to be genuine.

A number of management thinkers have long abhorred this continuing emphasis on the wrong kind of motivation. Harry Levinson, for example, claims that the prevalent carrot-and-stick approach to motivation of employees literally depicts people as jackasses—stubborn, stupid, willful, and unwilling to go where they are being driven.[8]

The implicit assumption of what Levinson calls "the Great Jackass Fallacy" is that the more powerful have a natural right to exploit the less powerful. What results is a continuing battle between those who seek to wield power and those who are subject to it.

Levinson says all of this is compounded by the pyramidal structure of most companies, with its heavy emphasis on internal competition for rewards and upward mobility. The end product is a system for defeat, with those who are passed over for promotion feeling increasingly exploited, arbitrarily judged, and dissatisfied.

Hardly a climate in which to persuade people to give their best for the organization!

Professor Frederick Herzberg of the Utah Business School regards the problem of motivation in its historical context.[9] He says people have been encouraged to make successes of themselves for five basic reasons:

- The desire for power to influence others and to control their own lives.
- The desire for a better life.
- The approval by organized religion and society generally of the successful person.
- The concept of social Darwinism, in which it was asserted that the most able survived and "made it" according to invisible and inexorable economic laws.
- The belief in meritocracy and the notion that those who were successful deserved to be because they were simply more competent than everyone else.

Herzberg goes on to say that none of these reasons seems to provide adequate psychological justification for the pursuit of personal success today. While they linger on as halfhearted slogans, they are not really strong enough motives to have much effect on people's work lives and behavior.

In Herzberg's judgment we need to offer a fresh reason for pursuing success. The one that he proposes—and the one which seems to be gaining support in American society—is the *personal achievement* motive.

More and more people seem to be satisfied when they are doing work *they* regard as important and worthwhile; and contrariwise, when they find themselves positioned between the carrot and the stick, they seem to be largely dissatisfied, restless, and resentful.

A New Reward System Is Needed

In my judgment there is a need to rethink the traditional reward system so that it is matched to contemporary needs and values. Indeed without that kind of matching, it is doubtful that today's corporate institutions can renew themselves in the ways they must in order to deal with the problems they face.

Adolph Berle, in *The American Economic Republic,* suggested that there is a set of qualities, which he called "the Transcendental Margin," that account for a nation's success and initiative. It was that creative energy, he said, which propelled our system not toward profits per se but toward beauty and truth. In a less sophisticated and cynical America, his assertion did not seem as strange as our times might judge it.

Author Adam Smith, an unlikely candidate for the role of wild-eyed idealist, says:

> If we still have it [the Transcendental Margin] . . . it should be possible to make work something fulfilling that does not need spiritual exhortation or economic fear to motivate it. That is a tall order and a big challenge, but the luckier of our citizens who have experienced something like it know that under those propitious circumstances it can be fun to bust your ass.[10]

When all is said and done, that's what the corporate system must do. It has to be structured so that those who are motivated to improve the organization and to make it responsive both to business needs and human needs are rewarded for their efforts. As Drucker is fond of reminding us, profit is not a goal. It is a result of efficient and responsible performance.

Somehow we have to devise a reward system that is attuned to the long-run best interests of the organization and everyone in it. Truth and beauty are difficult to reduce to particular and measurable corporate goals. But people who are motivated to seek them may be just what the corporation needs at this particular juncture.

One thing is sure. The crowd dedicated to short-run profits taken out of the hides of the worker and consumer alike has surely shown itself incapable of meeting our complex mutual needs in the late twentieth century. The one thing we clearly do not need is to continue to encourage that kind of behvior.

Isn't it silly to base a reward system today on the assumptions that

- The encouragement of intense internal competition is inherently good for the organization.
- Those who *appear* confident and decisive and seem to be doing things really are. (In the absence of valid measurements, appearance counts for a lot.)
- Any effective job performer is capable of the leadership role simply because he or she was good as an engineer, a salesperson, or a technician.
- Every manager will put the job and the company ahead of his or her personal life off the job.

Ironically, although each one of those four assumptions is open to serious question today, collectively they are basic to our organizational reward system. Once more, the maps don't seem to fit the territory.

What appears to be needed is a reward system which takes account of at least five things:

- The organization's pressing need to develop innovators and leaders if it is to continue to be successful.
- The need to encourage and reward those who *truly* make a difference, those who move the organization closer to its important goals while expending human resources wisely and carefully.
- The need to liberate people from whatever systems or parts of systems are counterproductive or prevent them from doing the job they are paid to do.
- The need to encourage people to continue to grow and to develop their talents in furtherance of organizational and personal goals.
- The need to keep people's attention focused on ways to improve the organization and the system so that the organization is responsive to human needs rather than always the reverse.

A corporate reward system for doing these things has not yet been articulated with any clarity for the organization of the seventies. In the next chapter let's see what may be necessary to help bring it about.

CHAPTER III

What Management Can and Must Do

Managers Who Don't Manage

IT is my earnest opinion that many of the woes which now beset American companies are traceable to managers who don't manage. By that I simply mean managers who are preoccupied with the maintenance tasks of their jobs. Because of prevailing day-to-day pressures, they busy themselves with two or three easy-to-identify job responsibilities and invariably ignore the rest.

Typically, they meet deadlines, they stay under budget, and they are not overtly disruptive to the organization. In the minds of a great many people, those three things are all there is to management. The sad truth is

69

that, in all too many American companies, all you have to do to get by as a manager is to perform those three tasks well.

But does the manager develop his people? Does he communicate with them in any consistent and effective exchange? Does he try to motivate them to be as productive and as creative as they can?

All those responsibilities have been seen largely as niceties for his consideration *if* he has any time and energy left over. But few senior managements in the real world of business have made any serious demands on him to respond to such things as *primary* management responsibilities. In fact, except in the most progressive companies, they have tended to emphasize the manager's role in achieving certain measurable business results while ignoring his responsibility for people development and management.

Neglect of "Outside Space"

British management consultant Neil Rackham makes the point that we have become very good at supervising the activities of people within given jobs.[1] We define the tasks fairly well, and we equip people with the tools to perform those tasks. But what worries him is our evident inability to manage what he calls "the space outside the job"—"the spaces" between people and between work groups, all the elements which are not directly related to the job but which may have an important effect on how well the job is done.

Some significant questions require answers:

What are the obstacles which prevent people in the organization from being effective in performing their work?

Are there cumbersome tasks or paperwork routines which reduce their effectiveness?

Is there for some reason a high anxiety level in the company so that from one week to the next, people don't know where they stand?

Is there any clear understanding of company goals and priorities?

Do people know in fairly clear terms how well or badly they are performing?

Does anyone pay attention to their development on the job? And on and on until we fill up the spaces between people and between work units of an organization.

The manager who does not manage is the one who ignores all of these spaces and concentrates instead on the more tangible issues of schedules, budgets, and order. In other words, he is the manager who tries to spin a cocoon around the job and the worker and who behaves as though only the cocoon is real and only it matters.

But he forgets that to the worker that portion of his work outside the cocoon is fully as important as the cocoon itself. The result of nonmanagement is an organizational climate in which people are often bored, anxious, ineffective, and alienated because the spaces are incomprehensible to them.

71

The Carrot-and-Stick Prevails

Most people who are moved into management are never trained to manage. They learn by observation and by doing, and unless they are very lucky, their models are about the worst possible ones for the task they face. A parent, a platoon sergeant, a cop, a martinet of a school teacher—these are the common manager models for anyone who is going to assume responsibility for the first time.

Harry Levinson says that if you ask American managers what the most common approach to management is, they almost invariably reply, "The carrot-and-stick method." [2] In a reasonably affluent and permissive society like ours, that approach is truly an anachronism. For some reason the conventional wisdom either ignores or is sublimely ignorant of the findings of the behavioral psychologists and management consultants who have been telling corporations for years what's wrong with their prevailing people-management techniques. Despite the spate of learned articles and books about people management, the conventional carrot-and-stick technique continues to be the most common approach.

The intriguing question is, Why is this so? There are several reasons, all of which have in common a misreading of both human nature and the corporation as an institution. Perhaps the primary reason managers are fond of the reward-punishment approach is that it is so familiar. When a child is good, when he conforms, he is rewarded either with approval or with material objects. When he is bad, he is punished, physically or otherwise.

That simple child-raising technique is carried over to an incredible number of institutional situations—schools, the military, government, the church, and a whole host of activities which profoundly affect our daily lives. In fact, if you really think about it, most of us are treated like jackasses for a good share of our waking hours.

So it should be no surprise when a new corporate manager reaches first for his stick and then his carrot when he takes over. The logic of the situation is even clearer when you recognize that he sees himself as being a potential victim of someone else's stick. He has been warned for years that if he doesn't deliver in some measurable fashion, he will be fired. Never mind that in most large organizations that's usually not so. The point is that he believes it and will act out his fears on those who he thinks can guarantee his success or failure.

The logical result of that belief is his inclination to treat people as tools to be used, bent, or broken for his benefit. The whole thing is classically simple. Keep them performing by rewarding them when they do what pleases you and punishing them when they do what you find displeasing. And that simplicity probably accounts for the popularity of this universally known and loved management style.

Not surprisingly, it is further fueled by the belief that this is the way the world is run. And God knows, there's plenty of evidence all around us that, whatever the theorists think and say, this is what *really* makes the world go.

The habit pattern is a difficult one to break because it is so ingrained in our institutional behavior. Also, because it provides for a system in which there are apparent winners and losers, it tends to feed the egos of those who fancy themselves the winners. In their role as managers, they are able to wield a fairly significant amount of power and influence over their subordinates, if they choose to.

Individual and Organization Losses

One especially disastrous result I have noted is that a good many people subject to irrational punishment by a marginal manager come to believe that the organization itself is largely hopeless. They interpret their day-to-day experiences with injustice and stupidity as typical of the total corporate body, and in large measure they give up any hope of changing it. The system is finally perceived as overpowering, and they freely acknowledge their impotence in dealing with it.

For the organization the losses are incalculable. Take the vital area of skill development as an example. The nonmanaging manager typically does not plan for further development of his people's skills beyond normal job requirements. Aside from the fact that he generally does not know how to perform this vital management task, he sees no good reason to do so. And amazingly, corporation after corporation puts no special emphasis on this need to "grow" people in the day-today work environment. That's doubly ironic because most people can be best trained for more responsibility on the job where the training is relevant to their real duties.

On another issue most senior corporate managements agree that their single most serious problem is communication. By that they generally mean the transfer of information down through the working levels of the company. But, typically, the nonmanaging manager does not see open and consistent communication as a significant responsibility. His attitude is frequently, "We already tell people too much" or "Why upset them with lots of information that they don't need or that will only confuse them?"

The result is that his people have no conception of the goals and the progress of the company, the goals of their operating unit, or their role in the total scheme of things. They are expected to shut up and do their jobs— however poorly they understand those jobs.

Results of a TI Study

Scott Myers has done a number of studies at Texas Instruments which show the impact of management style on motivation.[3] It might be well to look briefly at some of his findings. In one study of 1344 managers at TI, he devised a motivation index to separate the subjects of his study into three groups according to their responses to a questionnaire probing their feelings about their jobs.

In the total sample of managers from all levels of the

organization, he found that 30 percent described themselves as "partially motivated," and 30 percent as "poorly motivated." Next he asked each of the participants to select from a list of items those which described his boss's supervisory style. At issue was the boss's ability to inspire enthusiasm, the consistency of his expectations, his recognition of performance, his willingness to listen, his sensitivity to others, and a variety of other people skills.

Those bosses who rated high were described as "developmental" because of their effectiveness in developing subordinates. Those who rated low were described as "reductive" because of their tendency to inhibit initiative and to induce defensive behavior in their subordinates. A third group in the middle was described as "traditional" because, in Myers' judgment, they probably represent the majority of supervisors, who know enough not to practice reductive supervision but are not committed enough or knowledgeable enough to be developmental.

Interestingly, when motivation levels were contrasted, it was found that one-half of the most highly motivated managers had developmental bosses. Two-thirds of the most poorly motivated managers had reductive bosses. In one of the surprises in the study, both developmental and reductive supervisors were more highly motivated under developmental supervision.

For most of us in organizations, I believe this research merely confirms our own day-to-day intuition. A good boss is one who is approachable, who is open-minded, and who encourages us to use our skills honestly in dealing with real problems. The poor boss is the one who is intolerant and is always looking for someone to blame for mistakes.

Providing a Total Working Environment

But Myers goes beyond the question of the manager's style and emphasizes that more is at issue than ideal human relationships. The effective manager is looking to achieve organization goals through the proper use of human resources. To accomplish that larger task he must be equipped with certain management systems and tools. Otherwise he is trapped into building better cocoons without doing much about the support system for the cocoons—the spaces outside the jobs he controls.

In short, the organization itself must provide a *total* working environment in which the manager understands and articulates company goals. The individual worker is then able to match his personal goals to the larger goals of the organization. Of course, the company reward system must be such that he is able to achieve personal goals by helping to achieve organization goals. Obviously, all of that implies that he will have *some* role in helping the organization define its goals and that there will be an appropriate feedback and reward system not only to tell him how he's doing but also to reinforce that behavior which is useful to the organization. In a word, he will be involved.

At Texas Instruments and a few other enlightened companies, all of that is translated into planning systems, performance reviews based on the plans, attitude surveys, work-simplification programs, and inventory-control systems. These programs are all keyed to the widespread participation of the work force.

This mode of operation is obviously a good deal more demanding for both supervisor and subordinate than the carrot-and-stick approach. It presumes, among other things, that the manager knows what the company's goals are and that he supports them—a presumption that in most companies is naively made but which is frequently not true. It also engages a good deal more of the attention and energy of all involved in the process.

Ironically, anyone who has ever spent time in a reductive kind of organization will admit, albeit grudgingly, that it is a much simpler existence. You assume little if any responsibility, and your visceral commitment to the organization is usually only a negative one which leads you to rejoice at its failures and its clumsiness. Peacetime military service is probably a perfect example. You do your time with little or no commitment and only with an abiding wish to have it done with. And still there is a kind of mesmerizing tranquility about it all, an attitude of "What difference does it make?"

Commitment and involvement, on the other hand, can be draining and can lead to an emotional exhaustion for the person deeply engaged in large and complex organization tasks. Yet I suspect that if most of us were given a choice between being a jackass and a thoroughbred racehorse, we would make the more interesting and stimulating choice, even if it did make greater demands.

Peter Drucker, among others, has worried about the implicit dangers of manipulating people in the name of behavioral science.[4] It's a legitimate concern and one which all of us had better learn to guard against on a personal basis. But it doesn't justify (and for the record, Drucker never said that it did) the continuance of carrot-and-stick nonmanagement.

What it does do is to require us to develop a much clearer understanding of organization management and particularly of the role of the average line manager, for I believe he is going to have the leading role of hero-villain of this piece as our institutions seek to renew themselves to function effectively in the months and years ahead.

Needed: A New Breed of Manager

The occasion was a business seminar in New York. I was developing this favorite thesis of mine that the salvation of our corporations is largely in the hands of the ordinary, garden-variety line manager. As I was speaking, I could see an exasperated-looking man in the audience periodically making notes and slipping his glasses up and down over a balding forehead that was becoming redder by the minute.

When I finished and asked for questions, his hand shot up. What followed was a torrent of angry words with more of an attempt at a rebuttal than a question. As I recall the exchange, it went something like this:

"Have you ever been in a plant where you could

literally smell the anxiety in the air? Where people had bad breath, and where, if they raised their arms, you could see the sweat stains on their clothing?"

I acknowledged that I had known such situations over the years, and then my questioner got to the root of what was really troubling him. It seems that he was the director of a Canadian R&E operation with a branch in the United States. He claimed that, because of the U.S. government's Affirmative Action requirements, some five senior people who were retiring would have to be replaced with members of minorities or with women. The result was that some of the management people in this operation would not be promoted to a job which they would normally have inherited because it would be given to a black or possibly to a woman.

Clearly he felt this was unjust, and he was angry about it. At that point he posed a very important question to me: "How the hell do you expect anyone in this situation to work for change in the organization? How are the victims going to be motivated to reform anything?"

A woman in the same audience expanded on the question and offered her sympathy for the white Anglo-Saxon male whose life, she felt, was about to be ruined. I answered their questions with the reminder that the logic of such plans was to legislate what corporate management had not had the good sense and the good faith to do on its own.

I noted that yes, it was indeed true that some people might not get the rewards they had thought were coming to them. I even turned the question around and

asked them what real alternatives they saw to such legis-
lation, but there was no diverting them from what they
thought was the essential injustice about to be inflicted.
(Ironically, there was a notable and evident lack of concern for the injustices that had already been done to
corporate have-nots.)

A Demand for "Total" Fairness

Later, as I reflected on their anger and their apparent bitterness, another thought occurred to me. Here
was one more demand I've heard more and more of in
recent years for absolute organizational justice. People
today seem to believe that they must be treated personally with complete fairness by every institution. The
notion of the world as a place where there is a mixture
of justice and injustice, and where on balance most of
us do all right, is fading rapidly. And in its place is an
attitude which says that the institution has an obligation
to each one of us to give us pretty much what we want
and demand—and when we want it. Otherwise, it isn't
being fair.

As a brief and ironic aside, the militant minority
groups have used this tactic with great success and have
brought on the very reaction I heard from my Canadian
critic. It seems to me they do so with much more justification than most groups. But demands for total fairness from any kind of human organization are doomed
to disappointment.

In dealing with imperfect organizations composed of
imperfect persons, it is incredibly naive to ask for total

81

fairness. There will always be unfairness within organizations, and there will always be abuses. Unquestionably, those who hold responsible positions in organizations should be dedicated to detecting abuses and correcting them. But we all must recognize, as Solomon warned in the Old Testament, that the only way to give each person an equal share is to cut the baby in two.

The Need for Reformers

Perhaps one of the scarcest commodities in organizations today is the willingness and the patience to work from within for change. If we detect unfairness, if we detect what we regard as injustice, if we tire of trying to implement a certain scheme or a change in policy, we are too prone to throw up our hands and say, "The hell with it. That's the way 'they' want it, so why bother?"

And in the process the organization loses its ability to reform itself. My Canadian questioner was framing a position that is supported by a good many people today: "Why should I try to work for change when nobody cares about *me?* What's there in all this for me?"

It's an admittedly tough question which each one of us must come to grips with. Today, with more and more criticism of institutions and institutional behavior and even with the view that a given organization is guilty until it proves itself innocent, it becomes an even more compelling question.

One obvious justification for accepting what seems to be the thankless role of internal reformer is our collective dependence on our various organizations, whatever their abuses. A society like ours requires efficient institutionalized services to meet its needs, so, like it or not, large institutions will be with us as long as our society survives. The task is to improve and update them, not to destroy or do away with them, and anyone who argues otherwise is taking what is finally an irrational position.

A second justification has to do with the need for continuity in a future-shocked society. All of us need reference points as we go through life. Institutions which cannot grow or update themselves according to changing needs are doomed. Those people who have a vision of what we can become together are obligated to share that vision and to help our organizations adjust and respond so that they do not merely survive but will bring us through precipitous changes with a sense of connection between the past and the present.

The third justification for accepting the role of reformer is an extension of the second. Despite superficial appearances to the contrary, we have a greater need for one another's support than ever before. Our national obsession with privacy and our feeble attempts at rugged individualism are contrary to the social nature of mankind. Because of our mobility and our acquisitiveness, we have tended to emphasize the value of going it alone and seeking, though not really wanting, anonymity. Unfortunately, that anonymity has become all too painful a part of our lives so that the friendly smile, the gentle pat on the back, the kind word sometimes startle us as we make our way through any particular day. So used have we become to dehumanization, indifference, and surliness!

Somehow, for the sake of our sanity and for the stability and cordiality of our lives, we must change our organizations from the inside to reflect these collective human needs. In the case of the business corporation, I believe that task is shared by all of us who are part of such corporations but that it still falls more on the manager than on anyone else.

Change Agents with Promise

Since I have already identified the manager as a possible villain and because I said in the last section that he has not been managing, that last statement requires some explaining. What is needed is a new breed of manager or at least the assumption by the old breed of some new roles and responsibilities.

Of the three layers of management in an organization—top, middle, and first-line—I would submit that the most promising layer to take on organization reform is the middle one. I'll return to that point shortly. First, let's look at the reasons why top and first-line managers are not the best change agents.

In general, top management is not able to carry on the important process of organizational reform. There are several reasons. One is that top managers tend to be isolated from day-to-day events by their broad responsibilities and by the complex problems laid at their doorsteps. They are also physically isolated in semiguarded offices from the bulk of the people they manage. They are usually in the difficult position of knowing that something has to be done but simply not knowing exactly what to do or not being able to do it.

On top of all of that, most people now in senior management were brought up in an era and in organizations which no longer exist. They were taught to be loyal and to perform the tasks assigned to them. Their goal was to rise to the top of the organization and to cultivate successful careers in companies to which they would dedicate most of their energy and concern. Whyte referred to this group as the Organization Man, and though they are a vanishing breed in the seventies, they hang on in important positions in all of our major corporations.

It would be wrong to assert that they are General Bullmoose types untouched by the changes of the last 20 years. But in many instances their basic instincts are definitely tuned in to a more autocratic organization in which you simply tell people to do things and they do them. That kind of attitude very often comes to the surface when the going gets tough and they are pressed for results.

To complete this admitted stereotype, such senior managers often have little patience for what they regard as matters that are not properly the concern of the organization: such issues as social responsibility, the demands on the corporation made by various interest groups, the demands of women and of minorities, government interference in business, and on and on, to include a whole area of resentments many of them feel about their inability to manage the business. In the extreme cases they would prefer simply to overpower or destroy this opposition. In most cases they are not a very promising group for reforming the organization, since their instinctive view is that little reform is needed in the first place.

Similarly, first-line managers are not very promising for this important role. The young ones are too busy learning what management is all about, or they are preoccupied with their own career success. In either case they are not ready to work for change. In general, most of the older ones just don't go beyond the three tasks of meeting deadlines, staying within expense budgets, and keeping order. Survey after survey shows that most employees don't have much faith in their supervisor as a spokesman. And the same surveys show that the supervisor generally agrees with that assessment.

The likeliest person, then, to carry on the task of changing the organization is the middle manager. He normally has the experience and the maturity for the job, and, interestingly, he often has empathy for both the senior manager and the younger people coming into the organization.

An Ideal Middle Manager

A living example of the person I have in mind is Fred, a corporate manager now in his early forties. He took his first job in business in 1956. At the time he joined General Electric, the company was in the throes of its decentralization program. At a medium-sized GE department he had considerable contact with local top management. They were autocratic and demanding, and he soon learned that he was expected to get things done without questioning why. He chafed somewhat under this kind of direction, but at the same time he marveled at the efficiency and the single-mindedness of the operation.

In the early 1960s Fred joined a small capital-equipment company and got his first real opportunity to manage. He put to work some of his hunches about allowing people to participate in planning their work and in making decisions, and he discovered not only efficiency but commitment. One particularly important lesson he learned was the need to recognize a job well done and to deal with people as individuals.

Nothing very startling about any of this, but he was developing a style of his own. He was open and approachable with his people. There were few secrets. He was honest in his evaluation of their work, and he held up high performance standards.

In the mid-sixties he was squeezed out of his job when a large conglomerate acquired the small company he worked for. The few months he spent with the conglomerate were distressing because his new management had no interest in or concern for the people they had acquired. For the first time he had direct experience with real corporate cruelty. People were fired without good reason. Departments were arbitrarily reorganized. Career employees were demoted and sidetracked. The small company was milked, and long-term needs were ignored for short-term gain for the parent company.

87

Uncomfortable with the whole conglomerate movement, Fred moved on again to a large company where he felt he would be safe from the raiders. By this point he had ten years' experience, was 33 years old, and was able to contribute much more effectively to his new employer. The small-company experience had helped him to understand business in greater depth than he had earlier. Events were visible and responsibilities were broader in the small company. He was now able to impose that understanding on the bewildering and large-scale happenings of his new corporation. He moved with confidence in his dealings up and down the organization and was soon recognized as a real asset to the company.

Today one of Fred's great strengths is working with younger employees in helping them to understand and adjust to organization life. He is well liked and is able to get people to produce their best efforts. He is also able to win senior-management support because he understands their goals and their values.

Despite the frustrations of working within a corporate bureaucracy, he has never become cynical or jaded. Neither is he an Organization Man or a corporate boy scout. He has his moments when he longs for a simpler existence and daydreams about getting out of the corporate jungle. But overall he manages to hang on and to believe in what he is doing.

Because he is almost universally respected, he is able to effect small but important changes in his work group and, on occasion, has even played a significant role in helping influence important policy changes at the corporate level.

Fred is a real person I know. But I must admit that he's an exception, for too many people of his age and experience are turned off. Many have retired on the job. Some are biding their time until they can find "a real job" in another company. A few have dropped out. Some numb their senses with alcohol, and not a few permit their disappointments and frustrations to bring on early and terminal cynicism.

The picture is not pretty. And worse, if it does not improve, if we cannot learn how to produce and nurture the Freds of the organizational world, institutional society is in deeper trouble than most of us have realized. What we will surely face is a continuation of the sort of dissipation of the spirit which American society has felt almost without letup for the last decade.

In the next section let's look at why the middle is the critical level of the organization and what can be done to help the middle manager function more effectively.

The Manager in the Middle

Though middle managers are one of the organization's greatest potential resources, it is amazing how little constructive attention is paid to them. In the main they are left to their own devices and to their own definition of job responsibilities. While a good many of them complain about their lack of real authority and power, the facts generally are that the vast majority have considerable latitude in doing their jobs.

Ironically, the restrictions that do limit their actions normally are of the bureaucratic kind, the nuisance items having to do with approvals on petty-cash slips and the like. The important items such as planning, setting objectives for the work group, hiring and firing, and evaluating and rewarding performance are left, within reasonable limits, in their hands. And, of course, that's as it should be.

The real problem is not too much control or restriction of their authority, though that's the common lament. The real problem is lack of clear direction and of well-defined organizational goals. In a word, they are often adrift.

The Jacobs Survey

The extent and nature of this drift are portrayed in a 1974 AMA Survey Report, *Executive Productivity,* by Herman Jacobs with Katherine Jillson.[5] The picture that emerges in the study is a disturbing one. The authors note that most managers are not happy about their own productivity. In fact, 96 percent of their 1275 survey respondents believed that an improvement in executive productivity would have "a positive impact on the primary goals of their organizations." Nothing startling there, but the rest of the report shows that middle managers in particular know they are in trouble and believe everyone would be better off if they weren't.

The interesting and instructive question is how they define their productivity problems. And here the survey reveals that the middle manager sees a clear connection between his own problems in this regard and those of the organization as a whole. Fifty percent said a major cause of low productivity in organizations was a lack of well-defined organization goals and objectives. Forty-eight percent said the cause was "inadequate managerial leadership."

In clear and unmistakable terms they point a finger at their own top management and accuse them of not giving the organization a well-defined mission to which everyone can relate his or her talents. Not surprisingly, there is a crucial disagreement in the survey on this point between the chief executives of organizations and their underlings. The top man tends to believe that his subordinate managers are to blame. He says the answer is for them to improve *their* skills in delegating and motivating as well as their technical and market knowledge.

And here we have what I believe is the real nub of so many of our organization problems. Everyone is trying to identify who is to blame for the mess (an admittedly necessary interim step in correcting a problem), but no one seems to be moving to solve the problem.

And as Jacobs and Jillson point out, this *is* a significant disagreement because corrective measures initiated from the top and directed at middle management deficiencies will be seen as not dealing with real problems. If, for example, the president is whipping his managers to do a better job of motivating their people to achieve

company goals, the manager is more than a little cha-
grined if he doesn't understand the specific goals of the
company. In brief, his question is, Motivate them to do
what? To the uninitiated that situation may seem impossible, but it's not far off the mark in a good many
American companies.

The other causes cited by the managers for inefficient
and unproductive organizations are also revealing. A
third of them singled out "ineffective operating procedures" in their companies. A third also blamed poor
supervision-staff relationships at departmental and lower
levels. About the same percentages were critical of inadequate employee training and "poor morale" as causes
of unsatisfactory productivity.

When the managers were asked which company factors tended to make them personally unproductive or
ineffective, they cited some complaints rather familiar
to anyone who has ever worked for a large company.
By far their leading gripe was the absence of effective
in-house management training. They knew they were
deficient and wanted help. They also complained about
the time they had to spend on outside influences such
as those of pressure groups and government regulatory
bodies. The divergent work attitudes and values of
younger managers were also seen as a problem. And,
not surprisingly, they found office politics and excessive
red tape to be significant distractions from getting the
job done.

Ironically, in their responses, company presidents
tended to dismiss the notion that office politics and red

tape were detrimental to managerial productivity. But in companies with over 10,000 employees, 58 percent of the managers considered office politics "a serious deterrent" to executive productivity. Apparently, the perception in the trenches differs from that back at headquarters.

The study is especially disturbing when it is held up against declining U.S. productivity figures. For example, during the sixties the United States, among 11 free-world industrial powers, ranked *eleventh*—last in rate of increase in output per man-hour. Our gain was only 2 percent a year, compared to over 13 percent in Japan, 6 percent in Germany, and 4 percent in Britain.

What Must Be Done?

So where does all of this leave us with the middle manager as the person likely to reform and update our companies? At first blush it would seem to make him a pretty unlikely choice. He evidently feels misunderstood, misdirected, and misused. And to a large extent, he has been.

But that's mainly because he has interpreted the reality of his work according to the corporate dogma and because he has been willing to play a waiting role which translates roughly to, "When I see my boss behave that way, then I'll do it too. Until then, the hell with it." An old platoon sergeant I knew had a great way to say the same thing. When responsibility was placed on his unwilling shoulders, he complained, "All they pay me for around here is countin' cadence." Too many of our middle managers sidestep their responsibilities and their opportunities in about the same way.

The Jacobs-Jillson survey reminds us that there is no shortage of sound management theories and practices. The real problem is that organizations are ignoring these theories and running by a seat-of-the-pants reward-punishment method that has been discredited but is still commonly practiced.

In the authors' words, "We have available 2,000 years of philosophy, more than 6,000 years of religious study, and at least 100 years of psychology from which to apply methodological tools to the work of management. . . . The executives in this survey challenge us that it is time to forget the grandiose notion that managers naturally manage properly. We executives—from middle managers to presidents—need all the help we can get."

Specifically, what help is available? What can be done to assist managers in really managing instead of being mere straw bosses? The problem is a very frustrating one which defies easy and glib solutions. More to the point, it will differ drastically from corporation to corporation because each situation is different. Obviously, you cannot manage a large corporation in the same way Shortgrab Associates is managed. But there are some rather obvious things which need to be done.

Perhaps the primary one is to change the prevailing tone of fear and suspicion which oppress the people in far too many companies. This is a subtle thing to deal with because no one really understands why there is such a tone in the first place. I believe that it has much to do with ever-present but largely unspoken threats of punishment. "We" will reduce the size of your merit increase. "We" will lay you off if business slows down. "We" will demote you on the company pyramid if you mess up an important assignment. "We" will punish you for what we regard as inappropriate personal behavior and on and on. A favorite phrase in some corporations is "holding a man's feet to the fire" to get a job done. The choice of metaphor is hardly coincidental.

All of these things together compose a corporate bogeyman who is nonetheless terrifying despite the fact that he's a fiction. People act out their fears whether those fears do or do not have a rational basis. Despite the implied and spoken threats, corporate retribution is not a terrible swift sword. It's more like a tribal ostracism than anything else. The person who bungles an assignment simply doesn't get any more significant assignments. At least that's the way it is in many large organizations where it's usually possible to carry some unproductive people on the payroll.

Somehow this reality either does not sink in or else ostracism from challenging work is a far greater punishment than many people believe. Whatever the exact cause, vague fear of punishment is a destructive force in too many of our companies and in our institutional organizations in general. Think about the consequences. It keeps managers from speaking frankly against programs or schemes they sincerely oppose. It inhibits almost all sorts of risk-taking behavior. It keeps conflict buried so that it can fester and infect the whole organization. It inhibits creativity. It destroys effective communication. It discourages managers from developing their people for fear of creating rivals. And on and on.

Rather than a spirit of fear, what must pervade an organization is a spirit of performance. The test of any organization is its ability to gather together a group of rather common men and women and to manage them in such a way that they accomplish uncommon results.

Obviously, to make such an organization perform, people must be managed in a fashion that capitalizes on their strengths and minimizes their weaknesses. Genius is a scarce commodity, so the task of management is to place everyone in the job where he or she can best contribute and then to provide the opportunity and the tools required.

In the specific case of the middle manager, we must persuade him that the organization is sincerely interested in performance—that it is his special task to identify opportunities for the organization and to assign work so that people are focusing on their talents and what they can do rather than on what they can't do. The manager must also understand and believe in the values of the organization and must reflect those values in his people decisions.

And finally, it must be made clear that, more than anything else, the manager must be a person of character and integrity. People can forgive a manager many things. They can overlook bad manners, insecurity, even a degree of incompetence. But they will not ignore unscrupulous behavior.

The sad thing about Watergate was not the penny ante crime itself. It was that the chief executive of the United States contrived to hide the acts of his subordinates rather than disavowing them and turning out from responsible positions all of his underlings who were involved. The prevailing standard of behavior was not influenced by legal statutes or by ethics and morality. The standard was to bury misdeeds and to protect the evildoers. That is a standard that no free society can ever abide. Neither can any of its organizations of people mobilized for results.

So what must we do for our manager in the middle to get him to assume the real responsibilities of management? The broad brush strokes are evident; the tones and the shades will vary from organization to organization. But, in general, we must infuse the organization with a total spirit of performance. We must give the manager a share in the planning process in those areas in which he has competence. We must train him in the best techniques of managing people for results, and we must give him the planning tools and the information to do the job.

Perhaps above all we must select people with integrity and people with the ability to inspire others to want to give their best efforts. Such a manager, equipped with the desire to move the organization closer to its stated goals, truly has all the authority and power he needs.

James P. O'Neill, senior staff officer of Xerox, never speaks about problems or challenges. Instead he talks always in terms of opportunities—in short, identifiable customer needs that can be addressed and converted into results.

And that's really what management is all about—recognizing the opportunities, mobilizing people to address them, and finally turning them into business results. The carrots and the sticks should once and for all be consigned to their respective proper places—in stews and woodpiles and not in the hands of managers.

Should the Manager Manage People?

The easiest thing in the world is for a first-line or middle manager to deny his people responsibilities. He can do that by dedicating himself totally to the extrinsic task of producing a product or a service. He can do it by preoccupying himself with all of the restraints in the system which limit his freedom of action and his responsibility. He can do it by refusing to recognize the complexities of human organization and insisting that *"they* could change things if *they* cared." And he can do it by isolating himself from practically everyone who works for him.

All of these tactics, unfortunately, are so common that they are often regarded by corporate people as legitimate and appropriate management behavior. And sad to say, hundreds, if not thousands, of American managers abdicate their responsibilities in one or more of these ways every day. In fact, I would go so far as to say that the majority of such managers have serious personal misgivings as to whether it's worth the trouble to manage people rather than managing work. Because the corporate system has often tended to reward quantifiable results and to be largely indifferent to people results, their question is not an illogical one.

Richard Barnet and Ronald Müller, writing in *The New Yorker*, have stated the issue about as well as anyone:

> Our system of measurement reveals what we value most deeply. By what standard do we pace ourselves? By the number of goods produced and the number of times they are transferred from one hand to another? By the amount of energy we burn? By the amount of precious paper we accumulate? By the number of human operations that can be transformed to a reliable machine? By how well we conquer nature? These are the dominant standards of the industrial world.[6]

How the Humane Manager Behaves

The individual actions a typical line manager can take are obviously somewhat constrained by the system he works within. But he normally has a good deal more influence and power than he acknowledges, even to himself. Perhaps the critical thing is for him to behave as humanly toward his people as possible, to understand that they are complicated individuals with varying skills, needs, and ambitions and that they need him as a buffer against, and an interpreter of, the system. Without his playing this role, the system tends to grind mindlessly and inflexibly against their humanity.

Any institutional system is designed to stack people

up, trim off the protruding edges, and deal uniformly with what's left. The manager can collaborate in that kind of mindlessness or he can position himself between it and his people and administer the system in such a way that it will be as just and as human as possible.

Circumstances vary from company to company and will modify some of what I'm about to say, but I believe there are a half-dozen principles any manager who cares about his people will live by. To begin with, he will be a risk-taker. This is especially so with his own superiors. His first concern will always be with what is right and what is true rather than what is expedient.

Since his people and their interests are his special charge, he will stand up for their rights. But he will always recognize that management is a matter of responsible trade-offs, and so he will be willing to act in ways his people may not always approve of if he is convinced that the action is right and truly in the larger interests of the organization.

As a matter of principle, he will decline to manipulate people knowingly. Their dependence on him for recognition, salary increases, and administration of the work group gives him considerable opportunity to manipulate them. He will abstain from exploiting this relationship, especially if the manipulation is mainly for his own benefit.

The humane manager will normally put his own career goals *after* those of his subordinates. That may be asking a great deal of human nature, but to a certain extent he has already arrived. This means that he will be certain to encourage and foster their development and to promote their interests with his bosses. He is their link with the top and can greatly aid or handicap their movement by his reports on their performance.

In general, he will stay aloof from the intracorporate political wars unless he is defending the needs and interests of his people. Politicking for his own interests without regard for his people—or worse, at the expense of his people—is despicable.

In this regard he will be especially sensitive to the individual needs of these same people, protecting the weak and the vulnerable by helping them to identify and use their skills as best they can. The good manager is in the business of multiplying skills and compensating for weakness because most work groups are made up of rather ordinary people who can, and usually must, be stretched to meet the demands of the occasion.

And perhaps most important of all, he will show a rather unflappable personality. He will certainly not indulge in the tactic of blaming everyone but himself when things go wrong. Temper tantrums, finger-pointing, unconstructive and public criticism of his people are indulgences he can never allow himself. His job is to find out what went wrong and to correct it quickly and constructively. After the fact, he can and should deal with any improper habits or slovenliness that could cause a recurrence of the crisis.

Much of this can be reduced to rather insipid language that makes him out to be a paragon. That impression is wrong because some of the people who are best at managing and who meet most, if not all, of these prescriptions are rather rough-hewn characters. Integrity has a good deal to do with it, sensitivity helps, and maturity is a must.

The Ten Commandments of Management

Beyond this broad description of the effective and humane manager, I would list the following qualities as a kind of Ten Commandments of people concern and orientation:

1. Plan the work and inform everyone of the plan so they know what they're working toward.
2. Keep people informed about the issues that affect them. When in doubt, tell them.
3. Listen to people. All their opinions count for something and are important to you. If you have good reasons for rejecting their advice, tell them what they are.
4. Recognize and praise their accomplishments. Tell them honestly about their deficiencies.
5. Observe the common courtesies in your dealings with them. That speaks volumes about your respect for them as people.
6. Support them when they are right. Tell them when they are wrong, and help them extricate themselves as gracefully as possible. Then claim the responsibility for their mistake, if that becomes an issue.
7. Don't ever duck your responsibility by blaming the system. In their eyes you then become as impotent as you say you are.

8. Give loyalty, but demand it in return. An effective manager should never have to worry about being done in by his own people.
9. Always recognize that you do have the power and the responsibility to influence people who are both above and below you in the organization.
10. Recognize that the sun will still rise in the morning if you make a mistake. Keep things in perspective.

There was a time, perhaps, when all of this could have been described by the rather simple term "stewardship," a word which would have been easily and quickly understood. I doubt that that word is common enough today or that the concept is well enough accepted to carry the same weight it used to. But the purpose of human organization *ought* to be human development and the serving of human needs. The manager's task is to build structures in which people, acting together, will have the rights and powers of participation in the workplace.

Somehow that doesn't seem too much for anyone to ask of his or her life on the job.

Organizing to Get the Job Done

If it's not too great a strain on the imagination, let's assume that we have effective and committed line managers in place throughout the organization. Let's further assume that they are trying to engender a spirit of accomplishment. Typically, what are the forces that are working at odds with their commitment and intentions?

In most organizations it is difficult for the manager to maintain his commitment. The day-to-day experience of his work life seems to tell him that he is fighting a battle that nobody else much cares about. Even when he has rather clear-cut plans and is taking logical actions to implement them, there are dozens of small and large obstacles placed in his way. And worst of all, these obstacles are more often than not the product of the company's policies and sometimes conflicting priorities.

Even the company pyramid he works within seems to be counterproductive to his needs. It is too structured and rigid to cope with rapid change. It inhibits innovation and encourages job-defensive behavior which, in turn, encourages make-work. It pays the job and not the man, and its main people-control mechanism is coercion.

But in spite of all these limitations most businessmen seem to find the pyramid to be the best way to organize. It works and is easily understood, and despite its appearance of rigidity, it can be modified as needed. Does all of that mean we tell the middle manager that these problems come with the territory? Is he simply expected to requisition more baling wire to keep his piece of the organization together?

In a sense the answer to both of these questions is yes. But it's time to go beyond that simple take-it-or-leave-it response. In a simpler work environment, when there were fewer nonbelievers to deal with, that response was probably acceptable. But today—when the manager is supervising people who feel little institutional loyalty, who tend to be suspicious and distrustful of management intentions, who want their personal demands satisfied now, and who often measure results in terms of "What have you done for me lately?"—it is not acceptable.

The frustration quotient in middle management is simply getting too high. It's time to recognize that fact and to give middle managers the support they need.

Two immediate relief measures are needed. One, as I have been asserting, is to loosen up the middle manager's job, to stop bogging him down in procedures, paperwork, and red tape, and to persuade him that the real tasks he's paid for are planning and people management. We must stop the narrow definition and the close supervision of his work if we have any hope of motivating him. No effective manager worth his salt wants a narrowly defined job.

The second form of relief he needs is organizational. The exact nature of that relief is impossible to prescribe in any universal manner. There is no ideal mode of organization; there are only techniques which work as a product of varied and various individual company circumstances. In fact, if there is a universally applicable organization, it is probably the much maligned pyramid.

More Spirit Is Needed

The important issue is not really the structure of the organization. It is the spirit of innovation, performance, and optimism of the people who man the organization. Which is not to say that it's impossible to design organizations which can cripple effective and committed people. That *is* possible, but the odds are that such people will sooner or later correct the organizational deficiencies so they can do what has to be done.

The edge that our best organizations normally enjoy is that intangible spirit of performance, that belief in themselves and in the future of their enterprise. I believe that there is abundant evidence that we have lost some of that spirit in recent years. In my humble opinion, that is a tragic loss, because it has made us a people who look at the enormous problems of our time —runaway inflation, institutional decay, overpopulation, starvation, the decay of the cities, and on and on—and simply question our ability to do the job facing us.

It's a bit like undertaking any large task and studying and pondering it until we finally persuade ourselves that it's impossible to do and then never try to do it. If that spirit had existed earlier in our country's history, today we'd all be nestled in 13 colonies and operating small subsistence farms for our living.

The solution to our organizational problems of the seventies and eighties must begin with the spirit that we can indeed find solutions to the problems that plague us. The task is to modify our various organizations so that they are tuned to the unique company issues of the external environment the company is operating in, the work that has to be done to succeed in the environment, and the capabilities and characteristics of the people who will do the work.

Any company management which has analyzed its operating environment in this fashion is able to choose the unique organizational structure it needs to do the job. By the same token, any company that models itself unthinkingly after another company—even one in a similar business—is making a mistake if it does not make significant adjustments for its individual problems.

Spontaneous Incorporation

Let's take these factors one at a time. Most managers, and in fact most people, in a company tend to be preoccupied with their own day-to-day work problems as they experience them. Because of the necessity to organize and discipline the work and the workers, the rather spooky phenomenon of spontaneous incorporation takes place. By that I mean that the internal tasks to be performed, instead of being merely a means to a well-understood end, become an end in themselves. And soon no one remembers anymore *why* things are done this way. "It's simply company policy."

Our capacity to be distracted in this way is almost limitless. In a business this capacity soon causes a kind of organizational hardening of the arteries, which has been described hilariously in *Parkinson's Law* and in *The Peter Principle,* but which in fact is about as funny as a coronary occlusion.

Once this hardening of the organization is under way, it is very difficult to reverse it and to make people understand that the real reason for the company to be in business is to serve a customer with an effective product or service at a salable price.

The good manager is the person who always keeps

that fact uppermost in people's minds and helps them to relate their efforts to that goal. He is forever highlighting responsibility to the customer, or, if not to a real customer in the marketplace, at least to the user of the group's end product. In this latter regard, I have in mind staff groups who must provide a service of some sort to an internal line organization so that, in turn, it can better serve the direct needs of the customer.

Work defined and planned in that manner is disciplined by the task and is less likely to become impalpable. But it takes a good deal of persistence on everyone's part to so keep the organization on the straight and narrow. People are so damned distractible and often so far removed from the realities of customer contact and customer problems that they easily lose touch with the real task they are performing and the original need which gave rise to it.

People Treatment—A Key Issue

Beyond the organization's general market mission and beyond the work necessary to achieve that mission is the key issue of how people are going to be treated. In far too many cases that is a consideration which is given little time and attention except as it influences production or costs or one of the other elements of the corporate equation. It's rather difficult to persuade hardnosed businessmen that there are valid human reasons for concerning themselves with the welfare and the individual needs of their people.

108

The phenomenon of spontaneous incorporation of the work routine which I spoke of earlier somehow seems to make people considerations the least important of company priorities. In a crunch the employees in most companies can expect that they will probably be asked to bear the brunt of the sacrifices that must be made. Most people understand that and will grudgingly accept the necessity for tightening their own belts.

But, sadly, the history of organizations shows people being regarded like most other company resources. The individual is another piece of inventory which has a certain value, which depreciates over time, and which may have to be written off the books and scrapped as business needs dictate. A very revealing phrase in years gone by was "factory hands"—not people but mere hands which could be rented as needed.

Man's inhumanity to man is not unique to corporations. It certainly wasn't invented there, but it has often existed in both large and small companies where it has been common practice to manipulate people, to abuse them, and generally to ignore their needs or their rights. Those who defend shabby people practices usually do so on the grounds that there's no choice if the business is going to survive. They also point out that people have choices and that they can always leave if they don't like their work environment.

In a good many cases that is not true. People work because it's a necessity. And people usually "choose" their work not from a wide range of options but from two or three real possibilities, given their skills, their desires, and their economic needs. It is true that business has increased both the number of options and the mobility of the employee in pursuing those options, but for most of us the choices are still fairly narrow.

Hence it is possible for any corporate employer to treat people rather shabbily either by choice or simply through thoughtlessness. Personally, I believe that the latter cause is the more common one. It's like the man who truly loves his wife and children but who is so preoccupied with outside tasks that he neglects all but the most obvious of their needs.

A possible explanation as to why this happens was revealed in a recent psychological experiment. A group of theology students was asked to prepare a sermon on the parable of the Good Samaritan. They were given a very short time in class to do so, and then they were told to hurry to another campus building to deliver it to an audience. On the way they were purposely confronted by a person who seemed to be badly in need of their assistance, but practically all of them declined to help on the grounds that they didn't have time. The pressure of the situation had numbed them to the real-life needs of the people around them, and to the very lesson they were hurrying to teach.

Rather than being authentic villains, I think that corporate managers are victims of a similar kind of preoccupation with their job pressures. Reams of material have been written about people management, but it seems to do little to change the current situation in which people management in the actual work environment is really a rather low priority.

A Hopeful Agent of Change

John Kenneth Galbraith tells us that what he calls the "technostructure" of our society traditionally has had a need to override human personality in order to harness people to its purpose [7]—which is pretty much what I have been asserting here. Earlier generations have largely tolerated this. But, as Galbraith points out, we have for some years been developing an educated work force, made up of people developed by an educational system which emphasizes the worth of individual personality and independent thought.

Hence, Galbraith suggests that in emphasizing the need for education as an entrance requirement to the job market, the corporate system has planted the seeds of self-criticism and of eventual reform by people who refuse to be dehumanized or subjugated to priorities not revealed to them or even misrepresented to them.

The point is that this audience represents a significant and hopeful change agent for emphasizing human values and for reminding organizations of the need to pursue such values as a priority concern. What that means in specific terms in companies as progressive as, say, Xerox or IBM or in a smaller firm like Cummins Engine can be summarized in a variety of salient characteristics which compose the *quality* of work life:

First, there is adequate and fair compensation for the work being done by the individual.

Second, there are safe and healthy working conditions and generally pleasant surroundings.

Next is the rather intangible question of the oppor-

111

tunity to develop and use one's talents as well as to have future opportunity to grow and advance in the organization. There is the related question of one's ability to influence the organization and one's peers. In short, is it possible to have an impact on policy or even on seemingly small but important decisions?

And finally there is the question of how a person's job affects his relationships with his family and community. Does the job consume him and leave no time for other responsibilities, or does it enable him to lead a balanced life? And what of the organization itself? Does it recognize its responsibilities to society, or is it so irresponsible in this regard that its people are ashamed of their association with it?

These are difficult questions, but the answers to them tell us much about the quality of our own work lives and our self-respect within that sector of our lives.

Up to this point it may have sounded as though the responsibility for all of this belonged strictly to management. That impression, if it exists, is incorrect. Management has a vital role in setting the tone and the climate of the organization, but all of us have a reciprocal responsibility. In the next chapter let's look at where *we* come in, in the search for a corporate soul.

CHAPTER IV

What About Your *Soul?*

We the People

SO far this book has concentrated mostly on the responsibility of management to put its house in order. That's logical because management has both the motive and the influence necessary to change things for the better.

Realizing that, it's very easy for the individual to turn his back on his responsibility to the organization and to wait for "them" to improve his lot. Bigness certainly tends to feed whatever feelings he has of helplessness as well as his attitude that all this is really beyond his control. But no posture is more destructive of his freedom and of the organization's effectiveness than this one.

It's a fascinating study in human nature to observe how people respond to typical corporate internal pressures and frustrations. In practice, a good portion of that response is not really appropriate. There are far too many people in organizations today who are fooled by appearances and who therefore react improperly to their individual situations.

Why that is so is not too difficult to fathom. We persist in stating and restating the old corporate myths and the dogma until people are led almost to the brink of madness because what they experience is so much at odds with the myths. In their frustration they simply invent their own view of reality and then adjust their behavior to it. Their view is frequently as distorted as the one given them by the organization.

Offhand, I can identify at least eight different inappropriate responses which I have observed in a wide variety of typical organizations. These types are not mutually exclusive, and you may well see variations and combinations of them in the behavior of your co-workers, but I believe they are pretty representative, if not exhaustive, in any organization.

Bear in mind that we are discussing *inappropriate* behavior—not inappropriate insofar as it pertains to the individual's environment but inappropriate for the individual's and the organization's well-being. Ironically, at least half of the types I'm about to describe are often held up as role models by the organization.

Positive Role Types

Those people who respond positively to their organizational environments usually do so in about four different roles. Let me see if I can outline each one, put some flesh on it, and indicate what's wrong with it.

The Party Liner. This is the person who believes practically every syllable of the corporate dogma. He or she is usually a rather naive and pedestrian thinker who permits others to provide models of the work environment and then accepts them uncritically.

Vera is a good example. She's an executive secretary who accepts her boss's view of the corporate world without any questions or misgivings. If he praises, she praises. If he condemns, she condemns. In her mind the work environment is a nice tidy place where justice prevails and where the strong and competent win out. Vera is a vanishing breed found mostly among those over age 40, whose view of life was shaped by their upbringing in the 1930s and 1940s, when the world was much simpler and more tolerant and accepting than it is now. In some ways, the disappearance of the Veras of the world is lamentable because they at least had a faith to live by.

The Loyalist. Barely distinguishable as a type different from Vera, at first sight anyway, is Ned. But there are some real differences between her dogmatic assurance and Ned's loyalty. Ned is an engineer who takes the position that the corporate world is an imperfect one with lots of things wrong with it, but it's better than anything else he knows so he will give it his total allegiance, whatever its faults. Ned, like Vera, is not so common a breed as he once was back in the fifties when Whyte and others were studying corporations and calling him Organization Man. And every Ned himself is older and wiser, but he's still basically a staunch Loyalist.

The Insiders. The third type of positive organizational behavior is manifested primarily by persons who identify closely with the organization and who think of themselves as the Insiders. Because of their close identification—wherever they are in the organizational pyramid—they see the enterprise as partly theirs and themselves as having some tangible influence over it.

This group has always been relatively small because the day-to-day signals which most people receive from an organization of any size tend to emphasize impotence rather than influence. Any organization which can promote the attitude of the Insider normally finds itself the recipient of some very dedicated and conscientious effort. In fact, Robert Townsend says that the basic job of any organization is really to try to "come between a man and his family." The object is to get him "to enjoy his work so much that he comes in on Saturday instead of playing golf or cutting the grass." [1] Very often the person who regards himself as the Insider behaves precisely that way. Once again, this is a rather small group in most organizations.

A good example is Dan, vice-president of personnel for a small electronics manufacturer. At age 37 he has become a short-tempered, hyperactive executive nursing a bleeding ulcer. He looks ten years older than he is and was recently divorced by his wife of 12 years because she simply could no longer face the competition of his job. While his response to the organization is positive, the personal consequences for him are anything but.

116

The Insider frequently falls into the trap which has ensnared Dan and made him believe that the success of the company depends largely, if not totally, on his own performance. Some people can play this role without adverse effect on their lives or their health, but it is normally a great test of will and discipline for them to do so.

The Corporate Tiger. This type represents the fourth and final sort of positive response to the organization. Though the Corporate Tiger is a dedicated performer, he's usually rather disagreeable to his co-workers. The problem is that he is so aggressive and so ambitious that he often ignores the common courtesies and decencies of life.

Frequently, he is a young man on the make who watches with fascination the sometimes ruthless power struggles going on around him and does not comprehend their full meaning. The subtleties of such conflict and the playing out of roles are lost on him, and he comes to believe that rivals are really enemies who must be destroyed if one is going to move ahead. It rarely occurs to him that the foes may have respect and even affection for one another; he sees only the combat.

To some degree the Corporate Tiger is not truly a tiger but a 1970s version of the Organization Man—this time costumed in a tiger suit. But instead of being blindly loyal, he is often blithely disloyal to anything or anyone but himself.

Tim is manager of a branch office for a large computer marketing company. Like most of his breed, he sees his people only as a resource to be manipulated for his personal gain. He alternates between phony camaraderie and ominous threats "to keep people in line." Most of the people who work for him are afraid of his temper and his tendency to punish those around him when there is pressure or trouble. The Tims of the world do untold damage to the people resource in many companies until they are finally found out.

All four of these types are usually seen as responding positively to management direction. But each one in a slightly different way is manifesting inappropriate behavior both for himself and, ultimately, for his organization. Because his behavior *appears* to be beneficial to the organization, he often is held up as a model for others who aspire to responsible positions. In his own peculiar way each type has misread his environment and the way he should respond to it.

Negative Role Types

There are four kinds of behavioral responses to an organization which are generally regarded as undesirable or negative. In truth they may not be much more damaging than the first four we've looked at.

The Politician. One of the most destructive types in organizations is the person who is forever working out, behind the scenes, plans to improve his or her own lot. Unlike the Corporate Tiger, he relies on his human relations skills and his resulting popularity to carry off his pet ideas.

Shirley is an advertising manager in a medium-sized

118

machinery company. She's a very attractive woman with an engaging personality which she turns on and off at will, depending on whose office she's in. Her one obsession is finding out who has the power and the influence to get things done. Once she identifies such a person, she works long and hard to win his support and affection.

There is a trace of cynicism in her, but she really believes that the way to move up and get your own way is political manipulation of the people who hold power. Her main problem is that she is a complete pragmatist. The only issue on her mind is, Will management buy it? Her refusal to take any position until she knows what management's likely reaction will be is maddening to her people. The woods, alas, are full of Shirleys and their male counterparts.

The Escape Artist. Charley's solution to his organizational problems is to dilute them with alcohol and women. Convinced that his work is worthless to anyone and that he himself is a business whore, he does everything he can to blot out his work life. There are lots of Charleys in the corporate offices of the world, some of them in surprisingly important positions.

The Victim. Nancy is a perfect example of this type. She wallows in self-pity and is continually tuning up her already well-developed sense of injustice. The truth is that she's only an average performer, but she believes that she has been the victim of bias against women from her first day of gainful employment. If she has her way, she will convince her company that the next managerial appointee should be a woman and that she is the most

119

suitable candidate. Nancy is going to be heard from more and more in the years ahead.

The Corporate Cynic. Here is the person who has given up his faith in the goodwill, the good intentions, and even the possibility of reform of the corporate system. He stays on simply because he must make a living somehow. The task for him is merely to survive a day at a time. He has stepped outside the system psychologically and is so beaten and battered that he can only look at it with disdain and disappointment. There have always been corporate cynics; the alarming trend is the evident increase in their numbers both inside and outside the company.

Dick is a prime example of the breed. He has decided that the system is corrupt, immoral, and too powerful to resist, so he refuses to believe any of its pronouncements and spends his time protecting himself not only against it but against all of the people around him. His dislike and distrust of the system have been extended to all of his co-workers so that he is truly a corporate alien. He is also deeply unhappy.

Needed: Purposeful Leaders

Though I have exaggerated some of these characters, most of us can easily put names and faces to each of them, based on our own experience. This really is the sort of raw material which organization management has to work with and to lead in order to accomplish corporate goals.

120

The one fallacy all of these people share is their assumption that they must respond to the organization *as it is*. They have accepted the fact—or what they regard as a fact—that they are largely powerless to effect any changes. The task, in their minds, is accommodation of their behavior to the reality of the organization. Usually, it does not occur to them to try to affect the reality.

The real task of corporate leadership is to minimize destructive individual behavior and to persuade people to sacrifice some of their own personal goals and needs for the good of the whole. That kind of behavior is definitely out of fashion today. But the obvious truth is that the search for a corporate soul is akin to the pursuit of the Holy Grail until we somehow persuade people that the only way we can survive is by working together to make the organization human and humane.

The people sketched so briefly here are mere caricatures of the real people in our organizations. But they bear a very strong resemblance to the real people most corporations employ. Taken in this way they compose a rather depressing group picture. The one ingredient which can change this picture is purposeful leadership. And, contrary to popular opinion, that leadership need not be only at the top. In fact, the successful organizations are those which have leaders at every level from the maintenance crew to the president.

I've said elsewhere in this book that what we really need is change agents. Let's see next what kind of miraculous event it may take to produce such people.

The Care and Feeding of Change Agents

If I am anywhere near correct in my description of Vera, Ned, Dan, et al., it is clear that leadership-oriented management in any organization faces an uphill struggle. What it must do if the organization is going to be both successful and fit for human habitation is to take on the monumental task of persuading people that somehow they must rise above themselves and seek out work goals and values which transcend their individual interests.

And here is one of our society's major challenges, because a sense of duty and personal sacrifice, which is what we are really talking about, is not a predominant contemporary value. Indeed, the main emphasis of our society today is on "doing it my way" or on "doing your own thing" or other such words used to describe a turning-in on self and literally self-centered behavior.

And that is one of the major problems in reforming our institutions, because self-centered people cannot see the need or the sense in trying to improve any institution. They don't see what the personal advantage is, and they see little or no possibility of changing anything as corrupt as "the system." The implications of that kind of thinking for any free society are practically catastrophic, for what a free society requires most of all is responsible members who will contribute of their talent, time, and energy.

A Dominant Counterculture?

A really interesting question is whether we as a society have been conned into accepting values and goals that could only lead us down the road to despair. Think for a moment what has been held up to us as reality by popular literature, by motion pictures, by militant pressure groups, by pessimistic and sometimes befuddled writers, and by sundry other individuals and groups who constitute what has been labeled "the media." In the name of freedom and the right of the individual to live a life disciplined only by *his* values and *his* standards, these people have managed to intimidate the majority into believing that they must somehow emulate the views and the values of the counterculture.

That term "counterculture" is not a very specific one, but I use it in its literal sense to connote those values and attitudes which tend to be counter to those of the majority culture. Historically, the members of this counterculture have been on the receiving end of pressure to mend their ways and to conform. Today's tendency is not merely to be tolerant (as we certainly should be) but to positively endorse the values of the counterculture as appropriate for everyone.

And this is where the mass media come into the picture because, to a large extent, they have chosen to help legitimize these values by publicizing them and sometimes endorsing them. Seemingly, the outlaws not only have run the sheriff out of town, they have given everyone a gun and a case of whiskey in the bargain.

123

It is very easy to shake one's head disapprovingly at these events and to indulge in pious moralizing, but the implications for our society's survival are too serious for that. As difficult a proposition as it is, we must somehow restore a sense of balance to our lives without trampling the rights of those who choose not to share in the standards and the goals of the majority. But at the same time we cannot permit them to blot out our own rights to live without unwanted influences on ourselves and our children, whether those be a promiscuous sexual morality, an escapist drug culture, an overt or covert suppression of religion and spiritual values, or whatever form of coercion of conscience is used.

We are not victims of a conspiracy, but we are very definitely victims of our own cowardice in failing to protest or to resist that which we disapprove of. The "everybody's doing it" steamroller is one of the most difficult and most insidious pressures of modern life. It has affected our government, our family structure, our morals, our laws, our social relationships, our work lives—practically every phase of our existence.

De Tocqueville saw the dangers of this new brand of despotism over 100 years ago. He wrote in his classic, *Democracy in America:*

> The first thing that strikes the observation is an innumerable multitude of men, all equal and alike, incessantly endeavoring to procure the petty and paltry pleasures with which they glut their lives. Each of them, living apart, is as a stranger to the fate of all the rest; his children and his private friends constitute to him the whole of mankind. As for the rest of his fellow citi-

zens, he is close to them, but does not see them; he touches them, but he does not feel them; he exists only in himself and for himself alone; and if his kindred still remain to him he may be said at any rate to have lost his country.[2]

This emerging despotism of the counterculture and its values has untracked us. Which is not the same as saying we must repress that counterculture. In a free society we don't have the right to dictate to others unless they are clearly endangering the very existence of that society. But we certainly do have the right and the responsibility to express our disapproval, our disdain, and even our indignation. And that is a key point in this discussion, because the outlaws who have taken control of the town seemingly want to have their behavior not only permitted but also sanctioned. And worse than that, they seemingly even want the rest of us to join in.

Dedicated Agents of Change

What is the relevance of all of this to the basic question of this book? It is simply the fact that corporate institutions are influenced by the same pressures and value changes that influence our other human structures. Many of my contemporaries in business will write off what I am about to say as idealistic, and even as Utopian nonsense. But I remain convinced that our institutions can be reformed and humanized only by individuals and by groups who believe in themselves, who are dedicated to their mission, and who influence and enlist others in their work.

Many of those same contemporaries would argue that the times simply are not producing such persons. I disagree. The real problem is that such persons often *feel* cut off and alienated from a world they see as hedonistic, materialistic, and self-centered. Their agony often goes unspoken, but it is nonetheless real and debilitating. The goal is to provide them with faith in their ability to change events and to influence the people around them. The task is to somehow join them with like-minded people who can support them in working as change agents.

Psychologist Abraham Maslow identified a phenomenon he called the "peak experience," asserting that one such glimpse of a better way can be enough to give inspiration and meaning to one's life. This is what he wrote:

> Peak experiences may and do have some therapeutic effect in the strict sense. They can change the person's view of himself in a healthy direction. They can change more or less permanently his view of the world, or of aspects or parts of it. He remembers the experience as a very important and desirable happening. The person is more apt to feel that life in general is worthwhile, even if it is usually drab, pedestrian, painful, or ungratifying, since beauty, excitement, honesty, play, goodness, truth, and meaningfulness have been demonstrated to him to exist.[3]

All of us have had moving personal experiences of the sort Maslow describes if we are sensitive to life and aware of its events. Obviously, such experiences vary in intensity, but they are common enough to give us strength for the future.

John Gardner says there is indeed hope for those who would choose the road of action in reforming our institutions, alerting people to changing times and coping with their own personal anger and even their hatred.[4] Such a person, Gardner claims, does not indulge in holier-than-thou posturings but instead carries on a two-front war against those who would destroy the system and against the selfishness and apathy that block social change in this country today.

The vision Gardner holds out for such people is one of a commitment to the fight for a better future. He also acknowledges the frustrations that inevitably accompany that fight. The obvious question to be answered is why on earth anyone should subject himself to that frustration. And the only answer I can provide is the growing need of men to formulate and modify their values and to act on them in such a way that their lives have meaning. People want to believe that they somehow make a difference in their world. Influencing and changing that world, therefore, is a powerful motivator for anyone who wants to make a difference.

Some Pertinent Tasks

The individual who wants to help make any organization responsive to human values can hope to be successful only if he plans his efforts with some care. Obviously, his first task is to evaluate his unique position in his organization as well as to study the reality of that organization. You cannot affect what you don't understand. Therefore, the need is to come to grips with organizational reality and to understand it as well as it can be understood. That task, incidentally, is a never-ending one because such reality is neither fixed nor crystal clear.

Once one has become a serious student of his organization, his next task is to look at himself. Why is he striving to influence his organization? What are the real motives underlying his behavior? Self-aggrandizement? Egotism? Resentment? Hatred? The desire to do violence to the organization which he feels oppresses him? The fact is that motives of that sort are so negative that they will probably result in behavior which will be counterproductive to the real task.

That real task, which we should never lose sight of, is the need to make all of our organizations into fit places for human habitation. In short, what we are caring about and trying to deal with is anything which diminishes a person's freedom, anything which thereby makes him less human.

There is a danger in that simple definition because we don't all agree on what is oppressive. Obviously, we can never define that in terms which everyone will accept. So the apparent answer is for us all to take the positive tack of being for anything which makes institutions better suited to serving people and *against* anything which makes them self-serving or obviously oppressive.

We are still on pretty soft and subjective ground, but at least we have a guiding principle. In our permissive society there is sometimes a tendency to regard any rule as oppressive. That's a ridiculous position because we can't function without institutions to impose order.

The difficulty comes when the organization loses sight of the reason it was set up in the first place and begins to pay homage to its own structure and the perpetuation of that structure, without regard for the humans who are part of it or who are affected by it.

Such a phenomenon often takes place in large companies. People begin concentrating on internal work systems and internal policies and procedures and become so distracted that they forget they are in business to serve a customer. At that point the organization and its need for self-perpetuation begin to dominate everyone's activities. They forget that the original purpose was to satisfy a customer's needs and wants. One of my former bosses characterized that attitude beautifully some years ago when he used to comment wryly, "Never mind if it makes any sense. It's company policy."

A more prosaic example is the modern supermarket, which was originally created to make shopping for groceries cheaper and more efficient by means of volume buying techniques and self-service. Such markets have managed to cut food costs somewhat, but they've done it at the expense of making the customer an anonymous figure who loads up a cart with all sorts of bland, plastic-packaged foods. Gone is custom meat-cutting, gone is freshly received produce displayed attractively in bins and available for inspection, and gone is any semblance of customer contact or service.

In its place is a faceless crowd of shoppers who gather up a basketful of largely tasteless processed foods and then wait in congested lines to pay for them. A trip to the grocery store, which was once an occasion for social-

129

IN SEARCH OF A CORPORATE SOUL

izing and even some bargaining with the shopkeeper, thus becomes another dehumanizing experience for most people. The original purpose of the institution is lost sight of and perverted by the pursuit of volume sales and the movement of people past the cash register.

The individual's task in a corporation is to fight that overall tendency to dehumanize, in as many small or large ways as he can. And the small victories taken together can often represent a significant total change in corporate behavior.

Some Potential Pitfalls

The individual can indeed make a difference if he understands the nature of his impact on the system. The trouble with most of us is that we want sweeping and dramatic victories over significant parts of the system. Our action to humanize must, in our view, begin at some identifiable point, be carried out over a stipulated period of time, and end on schedule. Once that specific action is ended, we are ready to take on another problem. And at some given point in time we want to be able to receive unconditional surrender and to declare the war at an end.

That sort of thinking is bound to lead to almost unbearable frustration for the person interested in changing and reforming the system. Better that he view his organization in the biblical metaphor of the vineyard and himself in the role of the gardener who tends the vineyard by pruning away the dead branches and burning them. The task is a never-ending one, and it's a task

130

of encouraging the fertile branches of the vine while cutting away the dead ones.

The difficulty for most of us is to persevere in this task and not to turn our backs on our organizations. The signals from those organizations very often *are* discouraging ones. The conventional wisdom today tells us that one man cannot make a difference, that the task is so bewildering and so overwhelming that it is best for each of us to play his own personal game and to hope everything will come out right.

The trouble is that that wisdom becomes self-fulfilling. If enough of us believe that we can't make a difference, we will be paralyzed into inaction and our organizations will become more and more paternalistic, more and more rigid, and take over more and more of our freedom and our options. At the end of that road is the grave not only of individual freedom but of a free society.

Those of us who acknowledge and understand these dangers have an obligation to communicate our concerns and our restlessness to others around us and to mobilize them to work with us in the vineyard. One can easily question how that can be done in the midst of the frustration and apathy around us.

I suppose the best answer is that success will depend on our own personal dedication to this struggle and on our own personal example. People today need the inspiration and the support of one another more than at almost any other time in our history. Our rootless existence has led to a serious loss of a sense of community and of a sense of personal identity.

Each of us must recognize how much we are needed by the total society and understand the necessity to extend our hands and our convictions to those around us who are willing to join us in trying to make a difference. Most people today do not understand just how badly organizations need their influence and direction. We must make believers of them.

How to Create Believers

Ironically, there is no great mystery about how we do that. It's a matter of good interpersonal relationships. It's a question of our ability to care about other people and to show them that we care. People normally respond to any genuine expression of our concern for them as people. It is here in this humble setting and this humble fashion that the humanizing of any organization begins.

A Los Angeles personnel and customer communications consultant, Carol S. Gold, reminds us of a basic interpersonal communication requirement in corporations, and everywhere else for that matter. She says:

> Many of us tend to neglect the small but very necessary amenities that establish working modes among employees and influence the pattern of the day's activities. . . . Workers are constantly aware of the attitude of the boss. . . . It is a package deal, executed in a dozen ways. You listen when the other person speaks. You smile often and genuinely. You praise the person in front of others. You give deep consideration to the employee's suggestions. Learn to do this habitually and effortlessly and you have mastered a basic requirement of

management: gaining the respect and loyalty of those
who work for you.[5]

Once you have won the respect and the loyalty of
those around you, the task is to enlist their help in making the organization a more human place. That will
happen only if you share your vision and if you support
one another in insisting that people concerns must be
an organizational priority. The fight will be long and
hard for the simple reason that many people in organizations see people only as tools to be used and discarded
in accomplishing organizational objectives with efficiency
and dispatch. It will involve personal risk in incurring
the wrath of those who don't want their lives complicated by people concerns. But it's a battle that's so
stimulating and so important that it's worth all the risks.

Those people whose vision of happiness is a world
without care or effort, a world in which struggle is at
an end and where there is little or no seeking, will
never be successful change agents. The condition of man
is to struggle and the joy of man is to be energized and
refreshed by wrestling with his problems. The exhilara-
tion comes not with victory but with the uncertainty
and the excitement of the struggle itself. The victory is
never final but only the prelude to the next campaign.

The successful change agent understands that truth.
He also understands that there are things in human
organization that make perfection impossible. Gardner, the patron saint of all who would work for change
from within, says it best:

> The truth is we can look forward to no rest. We can
> seek and find; but what we find today will be taken for

granted—or rejected—tomorrow. And the search will begin anew. . . . The moral insights of tomorrow will make today's striving seem primitive.[6]

Working Your Corner of the Universe

One of the most debilitating facts about organizations is their almost sinister capacity to persuade their members that to struggle against their power is to tilt with windmills. Where you stand on that assertion depends on your own conception of the real source of organizational power. I've said elsewhere in this book that I believe we each assign power by giving our consent—usually implicitly rather than explicitly—to be governed by the organization. The irony is that after we make the assignment we often resent the bargain we have struck and we blame the organization for our feelings of powerlessness.

In fact most people believe that organizational power is an external thing, a phenomenon like gravity, which we can't see or feel but which is all around us, affecting every aspect of our work lives. The truth is that our own values and our own goals provide the source of organizational power.

The choices we make in our careers, as well as the ideals which guide our lives, determine whether we will be powerless or powerful in dealing with whatever organization we are part of. And here I don't mean to suggest we should be forever setting ourselves against the organization. That's a mindless and pointless trap which I've seen too many people fall into. The task is not to be forever against; the task is to help the organization serve people and human needs. What that means is that you use that human measure as a standard for evaluating your own behavior and the collective behavior of your colleagues.

Morality versus Practicality

A friend of mine who was formerly a management consultant and is now a priest clarified this issue for me some years ago. He admitted that in his business career he had made many small compromises but that he had never compromised one of his convictions. Of course, the catch is to know when you are in danger of crossing the line between a small compromise and an unacceptable one. Nobody can make that determination for you. It's a matter of diligence and personal conscience on your part.

Certainly, one key issue here is our own perspective. Fortunately, we are only one small part of both the problem and the solution. Since the total outcome of the humanizing process does not depend exclusively on us, our responsibility is limited to our own corner of the universe, which is the only place where we can really make a difference anyway. It's when we begin to believe that that task is immaterial or hopeless that we are in trouble.

Perhaps the words of Watergate conspirator Jeb Magruder can help us understand what happens when

135

we neglect our own responsibilities. This is what he said in a 1973 *Harper's* interview:

> I found that in the corporate life and in the government, it's best to do what your superiors want—as long as it's within ethical and legal limits. . . .
>
> At the university, you can sit and discuss alternatives. But if you're working at the White House, you enjoy your job, you've got four children, you're not rich—sure, you can leave and go somewhere else. But is it that important? So you subvert individual judgment over here to gain a more effective policy over there. It's the same thing in business. . . .
>
> You can't work in any *structured* situation without having this subversion going on on a daily basis. Most of the cases I can think of—with the exception of the war—*were not great moral issues. They were practical issues* [italics added]. . . .[7]

Perhaps the most revealing words are those last two sentences. This inability to recognize moral issues for what they are and this tendency to be "practical" instead are often characteristic of organization activity and decision-making. In fact, a good case can be made that our whole society is suffering from arrested moral indignation, with "right" and "wrong," "moral" and "immoral" becoming merely fuzzy words rather than limits of behavior.

The powerless person is powerless generally because he values something else more than he values his autonomy to act. "You enjoy your job, you've got four children. . . . So you subvert individual judgment. . . ." It becomes a practical matter to go along and not to resist.

Courage Is Scarce

In brief, you have assigned power over your fate by virtue of your decision not to take the risk of challenging a practice or an action you believe is wrong. And here is the major hurdle for most of us. We simply do not have the courage to challenge the crowd. Consider that if only one presidential aide had taken a strong and persuasive position in opposition to the Watergate burglary, he might have been able to prevent the whole dismal event from ever happening. The record shows that no one ever attempted that until after it was clear that the plot would fail and it was deemed necessary to begin covering everyone's steps.

The courage to take such risks and stand up to be counted is admittedly scarce in most of our organizations. And the intensity and depth of such courage are very often a function of the situation. Some people will be very courageous in one setting and noticeably reticent in another, despite the fact they may feel equally concerned in both. Other people may be so independent that they always speak their minds, and some may be so cowed that every statement is measured by the possible reactions of their audience.

What Risk-Takers Are Like

It's hard to say what causes the difference. Some would argue that it's the climate, the intangible tone which makes it safer to take positions in some organizations than in others. Certainly climate is a factor, but there are other things at work here. The risk-takers I've known were usually independent souls who shared several important characteristics, including a practically compulsive need to articulate their convictions in the hope they could influence the matter under discussion. They believed they had something to contribute, and they felt obligated to pass it along with little regard for who approved or disapproved of their position.

Besides this essential independence, they also seemed to have an inner strength, a sense of humility and earthiness that told them that the whole world was not riding on any of their decisions or any of their views. That quality normally made them much less cautious and much less aware of taking a risk in stating their own views.

And I suppose the clearest quality they exhibited was a confidence that come what might, they would always somehow land on their feet. The best of the breed always have given me the feeling that they would walk out any door, and tomorrow they would be as well stationed as (if not better than) they were today. Clearly there is about them an unspoken strength, a belief in their options, and an evident appreciation for owning their own lives. That appreciation transcends any narrow questions about the impact of any single action, recommendation, or proposal on their careers.

One of the finest bosses I've ever had was a marketing vice-president of a small capital equipment company. The company president was promoted to a significant post with our parent organization on the West Coast. My boss should have moved into the presidency, but he was passed over in favor of a younger and seemingly more dedicated engineering vice-president.

His boss had largely played it this way so Bob would consent to accepting a promotion which meant going with him to the West Coast, a part of the country Bob and his family disliked. To the president's surprise Bob declined the move on the grounds that his high school–age children simply did not want to go. Considerable pressure was put on Bob to move, but he refused because he believed that the family considerations outweighed his career ambitions and the prospects of a promotion.

Unquestionably, it is expecting a great deal to suppose that the mass of men can behave this way. Perhaps we have been so corrupted by our aspirations, by our commitments in the world, and by our belief that what we have bought cannot be given up regardless of the price we are paying, that there is only a fraction of the population who are reasonably free spirits. The good game has always been a lot easier to talk than to play.

The Price of Oppression

But perhaps if we reflect on the consequences of not owning our lives, we will reconsider the price that that kind of oppression exacts. Author Joseph Heller has his protagonist Bob Slocum describe his oppression in terms that fit far too many of our contemporaries. These are the words Slocum uses to describe himself in *Something Happened*:

I've got eight unhappy people working for me who have problems and unhappy dependents of their own. I've got anxiety; I suppress hysteria. I've got politics on my mind, summer race riots, drugs, violence, and teen-age sex. There are perverts and deviates everywhere who might corrupt or strangle any one of my children. I've got crime in my streets. I've got old age to face. My boy, though only nine, is already worried because he does not know what he wants to be when he grows up. My daughter tells lies. I've got the decline of American civilization and the guilt and ineptitude of the whole government of the United States to carry around on these poor shoulders of mine.

And I find I am being groomed for a better job. And I find—God help me—that I want it.[8]

And there is the tragic fallacy for most of us—wanting more and more and believing that upward is always better. Laurence Peter says it all in the foreword to *The Peter Principle*.

Man must realize that the improvement of the quality of experience is more important than the acquisition of useless artifacts and material possessions. He must reassess the meaning of life and decide whether he will use his intellect and technology for the preservation of the human race and the development of the humanistic characteristics of man, or whether he will continue to utilize his creative potential in escalating a super-colossal deathtrap.[9]

There is the real choice for all of us. To make this choice I believe that we must ultimately ask and answer at least three questions: Who are we? What do we really want from our lives? And what price are we willing to pay for what we want?

Those are deceptively simple questions. Working one's way through all of the implications of each one is a slow and painful process. And the hard fact is that there are many of us who are not capable of dealing with such introspective issues on the road to personal autonomy.

In the final analysis, I would suggest that the peace and freedom that the Slocums of the world desire lie in genuine concern for the human needs of those around them. They lie in the translation of that concern into visible action in ministering, in whatever way we can, to those who lie cut and bleeding in our paths from the violence done to them by the world in countless small and large ways. They also lie in searching for meaning in our own lives and sharing that meaning with others. And finally they lie in giving meaning to the organization by preventing it from taking over our lives and by reversing the trend toward private and public hierarchies that run mindlessly on and on because nobody believes they can really be resisted.

Combating Hopelessness

Columbia University professor Zbigniew Brzezinski has commented on the existence in the Western world of a deep cultural malaise that threatens two basic ideas which have provided us with our philosophical framework through the years.[10] One is the idea of progress as a consequence of change and growth; the other is the pre-eminence of liberty.

Brzezinski states that the notion is emerging that

141

progress means decay, that change is bad. The result is that more and more people are recommending limited or no growth as a way of arresting change.

On the matter of personal liberty, Brzezinski suggests that a higher premium is being assigned to the concept of equality—and not just equality of opportunity but equality of condition. The final product of these trends, he says, is a profound cultural discontinuity and pessimism. What is ultimately threatened by this cultural crisis is confidence, civility, and compromise. These three kinds of human behavior cannot exist without optimism, without belief in the future, and without belief in ourselves and our institutions.

Quite clearly, we must reverse this growing pessimism. The obvious question is, How? We cannot simply tell people to think more positively, but we can try together to develop a different thought style. We can encourage the best minds in our society to focus on feasible solutions rather than merely on the problem. The binge of self-deprecation and cynicism which our mass media have been on in recent years is a good starting point. This is a tired issue and a tired argument, but it's obvious that Americans are overloaded with bad news and with information which they can't deal with, either personally or collectively. The simple point is that if enough people attest to the fact that the sky has fallen, it soon makes little difference whether or not it actually has. What counts is that people believe that it has and will act out that belief in their daily lives. Feelings of helplessness are the first stages of paralysis. They are also fatal for anyone interested in working within organizations for constructive change.

An intriguing question that suggests itself is, What if we decide first individually and then collectively *not* to take the risks that are inherent in this role of change agent? What if instead we determine merely to turn in on our own concerns and affairs? What if we judge that the issues are too large and too complex for our efforts to have much effect and, therefore, we disengage ourselves from the very process of reform?

The interesting point about such a despairing attitude is exactly that it is an attitude. Robert Heilbroner and others have spoken eloquently and at length on the question of history closing in on us, of a feeling that there isn't much that can be done to resist events.[11] That feeling is evident today, and it certainly is sapping our strength to deal with our problems.

I think it's vital to remind ourselves that this truly is a state of mind that we are dealing with. What we obviously lack is a shared sense of social purpose and shared goals. Beyond that we are also manifesting a clear lack of confidence in our leadership and in our institutions.

Those are ominous perceptions and attitudes. And they are dramatized daily by our capability to communicate them with both power and speed through electronic and other media. Television, other types of instant communication, and our daily newspapers give us little relief from horrifying events which we are called on to participate in practically firsthand. All of

143

that provides a sense of turbulence and upset which becomes difficult indeed to face with equanimity.

The desire to retreat from life in such circumstances is understandable. The belief that life has become an impossible collection of pressures and disasters is also understandable. Sadly, such beliefs soon become self-fulfilling and debilitating.

Twenty-five years ago in Korea, four of every ten American soldiers captured died in captivity. They died not because of any horrible torture or mistreatment. In fact, on the whole they were fairly well treated. They died because their captors managed to convince them that there was no use in resisting. They died because there was an ingenious system of separating them and getting them not to trust or to communicate with one another.

The result was that no prison escape committees were ever formed. And, for the first time in American military history, not a single prisoner managed to escape from a Korean prison camp. What makes that all the more troublesome is they were rather loosely guarded.

It was not unusual in that war for healthy young Americans to throw away the rations of rice and some of the bad-tasting and bad-smelling food given them by their captors and, in despair, to cover themselves up with blankets. If they were left alone, they were often dead in three or four days simply because they had given up. Over one-third of them died and a significant number succumbed to brainwashing. The mortality rate was the highest ever for American POWs in any war.

This is a vivid and tragic example of what happens

when people determine that their lives are hopeless. It is also, in my view, a powerful argument against despair and particularly against the behavior it leads to.

Perhaps what we must learn to do is to brush aside these oppressive feelings and to live our lives on the simpler and more immediate level of our own experience. The gravity of the long-term future *can* be disruptive and discouraging, but the truth is that all of us live our real lives on a fairly basic, fairly simple day-to-day level.

If we are to preserve our sanity, to achieve a reasonable degree of personal peace, and to grapple with the problems of our lives, we must somehow learn to live with purpose, with courage, and with some degree of optimism.

So the "what if" questions and the option of isolating ourselves and turning in on our own problems and affairs simply do not seem workable. Somehow we must find a different solution. I believe that solution is to accept the role of change agent—at least in our own corners of the universe.

Good Leaders and Good Followers

There is one final quality which any change agent must possess and which, more and more, we in American society seem to devalue. It has a variety of names, all of which are rather high sounding and abstract. Some people call it "responsibility"; others describe it as "integrity" or simply as "decency." Whatever the word, what we are groping to define is a sense of per-

145

sonal honesty and responsibility—the person whose word means something, whose promises will be kept, whose opinions are expressed sincerely and forthrightly.

Such qualities were once regarded as the essential elements of leadership, but leadership is a sore subject these days. There is an obvious lack of confidence in governmental and other institutional leaders. Even the president of the United States is regarded as doing well in the polls in any given week when 40 or 50 percent of the people express confidence in his leadership.

Leadership crises are as old as recorded history. We should not forget that followers tend to be fickle in their allegiance. But it is too easy to blame such crises and to blame our leaders for every problem we face. It is too easy to abdicate our own personal responsibility for what ails us.

Any effective organization requires leaders who truly know how to lead. They must be people who deserve our trust, who inspire us, who lift our sights, and who bring us together in a common cause. The other side of that issue is that such leaders have a right to expect loyalty and support from the people they are leading.

And that is a major problem of our time, because such loyalty and support are in short supply. While we may complain with some legitimacy about the quality of contemporary leaders, our followership also leaves much to be desired. We are too often suspicious, distrusting, cynical, and self-serving followers. The relationship between leader and led should be one of mutual concern and mutual support.

And yet the reality is usually quite different. Even the most perfect of all leaders, Jesus Christ, had leadership crises. He was doubted and misunderstood by his followers, the closest of whom denied him and betrayed him in the end. And during his ministry, his disciples frequently challenged his judgment and urged him to rethink his decisions. But finally, they were able to overcome their lack of confidence and to obey his simple command to "Follow me." And in the end most of them, according to the traditions passed down to us, died as martyrs to the faith their leader had given them.

Much has been said and written about good leadership. A great deal less has been said about the qualities of the good follower. Intuitively, however, we know a good deal about those qualities even if we don't always evidence them. The good follower is generous. He is loyal, and he is even-tempered and imperturbable. What he should not be is selfish, envious, and bitter.

But again the reality of our lives is that competition for material gain or for status—or simply the orneriness of human nature—often brings to the forefront the very qualities which destroy good followership. What is even worse is that these same qualities which make us think first of *our own* welfare and *our own* needs tend also to isolate us from others and to produce in us the sense of separation and alienation which makes life a rather dismal business these days.

Self-centered and alienated people are usually pretty unpleasant people to have around. Too much of their time and energy is expended in self-pity and self-service

147

to make them useful members of any enterprise which requires cooperation and mutual concern.

Alienation is a destructive posture. People who feel oppressed and dehumanized take out their anger on both the organization and on their peers, frequently failing to distinguish between them. For the organization, that means outright or subtle sabotage of its objectives. For the individual, that means acts of aggression committed against those around him or hypersensitivity and defensiveness in his dealings with co-workers. In practically all cases it means an intensification of selfishness and bitterness. The result normally is a dilution of performance, the one real measure of both effective leadership and effective followership.

How we end up, then, is with a truth so basic that it hardly seems worth stating. The performance of any organization requires both those who lead and those who are led to acknowledge and manifest their mutual obligation, their mutual interest, and their mutual regard. Like all basic truths, this one is all too easy to ignore. And yet if we ignore it, we do so at our own expense and peril.

Realistic Expectations

One of the great hazards faced by anyone who would try to humanize any large organization is the danger of disillusionment and what that can do to his staying power. We often behave as though idealism or cynicism

148

were the only two possible attitudes in dealing with our organizations.

That assumption tends to polarize our job behavior and to make us deal with one another in absolute terms which block understanding and tolerance. One of the problems is that our notions of reform are based on Utopian visions. It is practically an article of faith in our cultural heritage that we clear away the debris of one disaster and then begin the reforming process in such a way that all the old mistakes and omissions will be corrected and never repeated.

Americans love new beginnings. Given our national history and our pioneer tradition, that love is at least understandable. But it is terribly unrealistic in that it ignores the imperfect nature of humankind.

The "Repeal" of Original Sin

Some years ago we could have described the imperfection according to the doctrine of original sin and human corruptibility. Today we have tried to repeal that doctrine in our own thinking about ourselves. Bishop Fulton J. Sheen has commented wryly that it used to be only Catholics who believed in the Immaculate Conception. Now, he says, the whole world believes in its own Immaculate Conception.

Ironically, the repeal of the doctrine of original sin was seen as a way for us to gain better insights into our real selves without the handicap of "superstition." Instead it has tended to lead us to a rather formless vision of human life in which the forces of good and evil become only relative notions and each one of us is left to work out a personal morality and ethics according to his own views and desires.

It would be hard to think of a formula more likely to bring down upon us feelings of frustration, guilt, and failure. Alas, in the real world most of us are not equipped to make such judgments without a framework or without guidelines of some kind.

My wife's immigrant grandmother had a graphic way to express her healthy skepticism about human nature. In speaking about potential mates for her children or her grandchildren, she invariably observed, "Ah, they walk down the aisle with one face, and they come back with another." The observation was not bitter. It was merely a statement of the facts of human nature as she saw them.

Michael Novak asserts there will truly be new beginnings in American life when we stop preaching falsely at one another. It is an imperfect world, he reminds us, in which it is discouraging to be a teacher, a lawyer, or even a movie star, and in which "carpenters get corners wrong and doctors work with probabilities."

The obvious lesson in dealing with our organizations is that we must not lose sight of some basic truths. The reformed and renewed institution will produce both good and evil simultaneously. Our job is to identify and deal honestly with the evil. The reformers probably will be tainted by their new power and may even become the new oppressors. We must not give up reform; we must continue it and drive out the inevitable new gang of oppressors.

This continuing need for vigilance in reforming and renewing our institutions makes those who long for and search for Utopia practically despondent. The problem is not necessarily the institution or the people who now control it. The problem is corruptible human nature and the ways in which that corruptibility is reflected in our various organizations.

The Threat of Pessimism

Having said that, I wish to emphasize what I personally regard as an even greater threat to institutional renewal than Utopian longings. That threat is the pessimism of atheistic existentialism as defined by such people as Jean-Paul Sartre and Albert Camus. Their beliefs that there is no universal moral law and that there are no absolute moral values have had a profound influence on contemporary man.

Camus' doctrine of the absurd, in which he asserts that we live in a meaningless universe which renders human hopes and desires absurd, has been particularly influential. American writers and intellectuals who have embraced these notions and reflected them in their own work have, in turn, influenced large numbers of Americans to believe that our disordered and sometimes tragic world justifies their being responsible only to themselves. Their mission is to use their freedom to face life's absurdity as bravely as they can.

Such a pessimistic view of life is bound to lead the mass of men to a neo-utilitarianism in which the seeking after pleasure and the avoidance of pain become primary human goals. More to the point, people who believe the universe is meaningless and that human hopes are futile are capable of reforming nothing. Instead, the focus of their lives is on "getting what's coming to them."

There is a brighter side to existentialist doctrine which emphasizes faith and the use of man's freedom to rediscover love, fidelity, and hope. But that view has had much less popular impact than the doctrine of the absurd.

My point is that American society has drunk deeply from the stream of French existentialism. Wittingly and unwittingly, we have all been infected to a greater or lesser degree by this philosophical nihilism, this pessimism which has tended to rivet our attention on our own personal needs practically to the exclusion of anything else.

Such a view of life is shattering. Few of us have the inclination or the strength to go it alone, to lead a life cut off from hope and anesthetized to the needs and the humanity of others. That is alienation of the worst sort, and it cannot help but lead us to a despair whose end is personal and collective decadence.

No one can or will work to change our organizations unless he is motivated by a vision of human possibility. For some that is a faith in God and in the dignity and worth of man. For others that vision of human possibility is a product of their sincere humanism or perhaps even of the practical need to make their lives within organizations bearable. Whatever the motive, the vision of human possibility is essential to those who would work as change agents in our organizations.

The Need for Realism

That work requires us to be realistic without being cynical and to recognize that the task is never finished. Informed and healthy realism is in short supply today. Instead we become the victims of our wish for perfection on the one hand and our despair on the other. Understanding that fact and acting on it make up the first step toward avoiding the roller-coaster highs and lows that we individually and collectively are subject to.

In corporate life I am continually perplexed by the naiveté of people who believe that a reorganization or a management change will solve problems magically. Or the people who are persuaded that the mere formulation and announcement of a policy will suitably alter human behavior. These things may be necessary in the day-to-day operation of the business, but they will not lead us to perfection.

That conclusion may well prompt us to ask one more time, Then why bother? The answer, one more time, is that if we don't work to perfect our organizations, they will deteriorate to the lowest levels of human corruptibility. Perhaps there is a good analogy in the job of the homemaker. That job is never completed. The kitchen is in disarray after each meal, the beds are unmade each morning, the dust collects on every flat

153

surface without letup, the sinks and toilets have to be scrubbed week in and week out, and the soiled clothing is piled in hampers to be recycled day in and day out. And yet homemakers face these tasks anew each day, admittedly with varying degrees of enthusiasm. The rhythm of life demands that they do the same old jobs over and over. We in our more status-conscious organizations are not so far removed from this kind of rhythm as we like to think. Like the diligent homemaker, we work against the demands and the obstacles in the knowledge that they will return tomorrow in pretty much the same form.

In corporations we are probably the most susceptible to the Utopian aspiration in our management thinking. I have always been troubled by a particular passage of Douglas McGregor's classic book, *The Human Side of Enterprise,* in which he contrasts the characteristics of a Theory X organization (an autocratically styled management) versus a Theory Y organization (a participative team-type management style).[12] In the Theory X organization, people are generally seen as indifferent, domineering, sullenly disagreeable, afraid of conflict, and largely without mutually understood direction. All of this, persumably, is the behavior which autocracy alone evokes.

In contrast, in the Theory Y organization, people are enthusiastic, tolerant, able to compromise their differences, free to express their feelings, and interested in the general welfare of the group. McGregor was a brilliant observer and consultant, and he spent several years explaining and clarifying his Theory X, Theory Y

154

descriptions of organizational behavior. But his work has been muddied by those who would see the two theories as options for management. He saw them as descriptions of organizations in action, not as prescriptions.

The difficulty with the Theory X, Theory Y constructs is that one can be read as Utopia and the other as Hell, tending to perpetuate the notion of the bad guys versus the good guys and of a right and a wrong way to manage humans in an organization. The trouble is that the McGregor equation has no term for original sin, unless it is X.

We are all painfully aware of how difficult it is actually to be what we want to be in our personal lives. On the personal road each one of us travels, we falter, stumble, and sometimes fall flat on our faces. But somehow we stagger to our feet and go on, more or less in cadence with our ideals and our hopes, until we break stride again and repeat the process. If it is that hard for us to do this individually, why do we expect so much more from our organizations, which after all reflect our collective virtues and vices?

All of our institutional organizations today are threatened by unrealistic demands and by our tendency to presume them guilty until they prove otherwise. That historic shift in attitude has prompted managers in many corporations and organizations to preoccupy themselves with forestalling and coping with attacks from both the inside and the outside of their organizations.

More and more we are imposing our unrealistic expectations on institutional management and then castigating it when those expectations are not fulfilled. Separating ourselves from our organizations and then turning them into scapegoats in the battle to get what we think we have coming are about as good a way as man has ever invented to bring about their destruction —and maybe his own.

CHAPTER V

Some Final Matters

But How About the Bottom Line?

THERE'S a curious either/or proposition which is accepted almost as an article of faith by people in corporate organizations. It assumes that efficiency, productivity, and high profits are on one end of an imaginary scale and that concern for employees and their participation in planning and decision-making are on the other. According to this particular view of the corporate process, anything done to improve the employee's lot or to permit him to participate in the system will be done, by definition, at the expense of efficiency, productivity, or profits—or all three.

The origins of this mentality can probably be traced to the familiar carrot-and-stick management of people. Although this view is simplistic and largely wrong, it still guides the behavior of a good many responsible people in our business organizations. Deep down they believe that the best way to get results is through fear and punishment and that if you spare the whip, you spoil the business.

It is true that there are points of conflict between an individual's needs and the larger needs of the organization. But there are a good many more points where the two sets of needs correspond. The person who argues that if we humanize organizations, we will produce groups of lotus-eaters who forget why they were hired is as incorrect as the person who claims that humanization will lead to great improvement in morale and, therefore, great increases in productivity. There simply is no clear cause-effect relationship. If we are worried about humanizing organizations, we worry about it as a worthy end in itself and not merely as a means to some other unstated end.

Alas, that argument seems to do little to sway managers who are under pressure to meet very specific profit goals or sales results or shipping dates or whatever the bogey happens to be for the work group.

Developing a Realistic Model

Having admitted that there is not a clear cause-effect relationship between people concerns and business concerns, to use the terms which commonly describe this dichotomy, let's try to develop a more realistic model of the forces we are looking at.

Perhaps the best way to view the problem is to look at the two overlapping universes of employee needs and organization needs in the accompanying illustration.

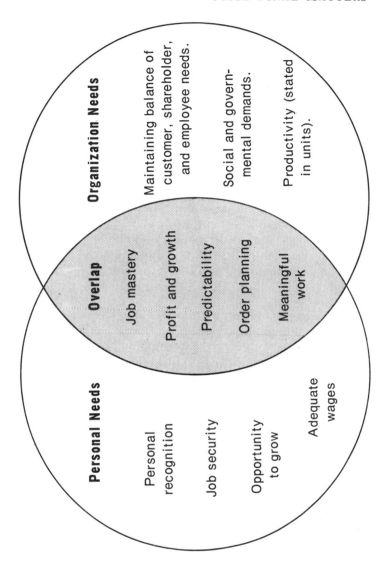

In this model the people-needs universe, which is primarily a list of the individual's personal concerns, includes four major issues. These are impossible to rank, although it is clear that two of them—job security and adequate wages—must be present before the individual worries much about the other two. Once he has a reasonably dependable job which pays him what he regards as adequate wages, then he tends to concern himself with growth and the opportunity to climb his particular job ladder.

That interest, of course, varies in intensity from individual to individual and from work group to work group. As a generalization, for example, sales and marketing people tend to be more concerned with the opportunity for upward mobility than do engineers. But the desire to see some kind of movement in one's career is fairly universal.

Probably the most pressing noneconomic people need is recognition. Practically everyone wants to hear some occasional praise and some expression of his value to the enterprise. When that verbal praise is reinforced with more tangible material rewards, it is all the more effective.

While the organization has an interest in all four of these people needs, its interest is usually much less intense than that of the individual employee. Wise management does recognize, however, that satisfying people needs, to the extent that it is possible to do so, is a sensible business practice.

On the other hand, the organization has some needs

of its own which sometimes seem to conflict with people needs. To begin with, the practice of management is the practice of responsible trade-offs to keep the organization healthy and productive. Besides the employee, management must worry first and foremost about the customer. The simple fact is that without satisfied customers the business collapses.

Further, there are the needs of shareholders. The capital they provide is essential to the business. Their expression of faith in the business is an important measure of the public's regard for management's performance. And business results stated in earnings per share are generally regarded as a meaningful measure of business performance.

Any effective senior management is looking to customer performance and to stock performance as major concerns to be balanced against employee needs. The trade-offs are sometimes painful, and the truth of the matter is that, historically, the employee has been low man on this particular totem pole. If there was a real crunch, he was the one who could expect to be squeezed the hardest.

The reason is simply that senior management can be called to account in very painful ways by both the shareholders and the customers. The shareholders can express their unhappiness by selling their shares or refusing to buy additional shares, thus making it difficult for management both directly and indirectly (i.e., favorable borrowing posture) to raise new capital. The power held by large numbers of unhappy and angry customers is too obvious to require much explanation. Aside from labor organizations, the employee is hard put to make known his complaints with the same force as customers or shareholders.

So the employee remains the most vulnerable in terms of his expendability in bad times and his dependence on the organization for a paycheck. Another pressure which is exerted directly on the employee is the organization's need for optimum productivity levels. High employee productivity tends to improve profit performance simply by reducing the unit production costs of any product.

The trouble is that people have believed that productivity is something which can be improved merely through exhortations to work harder or by speeding up the assembly line. That subject is beyond the scope of this book, but certainly we should have learned by now that what Herzberg calls the "KITA (kick in the ass) theory" of motivation is a bankrupt way of looking at productivity. Higher rates of productivity are much more a function of automation, intelligent management decisions, and efficient work flow than they are of increased human effort.

Areas of Conflict

Admittedly, there is some tension and some conflict between organization needs and people needs. But to return to the point at the beginning of the chapter, it is certainly not the either/or tug-of-war which many people have asserted it is.

162

Some observers have carried this last point to its extreme and have suggested that there is *no* conflict: that worker and management are in this thing together and that whatever action benefits the larger organization and contributes to its health is beneficial to all. Certainly there is more than a grain of logic in that premise. Where it breaks down is in the distribution of the organization's largess. Generally, the employee has been given a much smaller share of the wealth in return for his effort and dedication than has management or even the shareholder, at least if we are speaking in proportion to dedication and effort.

A relatively new element in the organization's responsibilities is social and governmental demands. There are great pressures today on companies to share their wealth, to put something back into the society at large. Whether we are talking about grants to museums and civic organizations or scholarships for impoverished or underprivileged children, the corporation more and more is being asked to devote a share of its profits to worthy causes.

Beyond that kind of demand, the corporation is also receiving from the government much more scrutiny of its hiring and its people practices generally. Affirmative Action plans must be a way of life for any company which wants to do business with government units and agencies. These plans require specific and well-coordinated policies to protect minorities, women, and older workers from any intentional or unintentional employer discrimination.

163

Overlapping Interests

Despite some of the seeming areas of conflict between people needs and organization needs, there is also a third area of *overlapping* interests. Both groups, for example, are concerned about—or should be concerned about—profit, because it is the measure of the enterprise's success in meeting customer needs.

Both groups should care about order and effective planning. Admittedly, they may see those issues from different perspectives and may not agree on what they mean, but they certainly should agree on their necessity if the organization is to be successful.

Similarly, the issues of providing meaningful work and job predictability are common organization and people needs. Once again, the perspectives on those issues may be somewhat different, but certainly there is no quarrel over the necessity for a predictable work environment or for real work that is of some value to the organization.

And, finally, there is the issue of job mastery. This is one of the most basic of all employee needs. Every employee must successfully master his work responsibilities if he is to have any hope of job satisfaction. And it certainly is imperative to the organization that everyone be as proficient as possible at his job.

But all of this does not answer the assertion that attention to people needs will adversely affect bottom-line results. Perhaps the best answer is not to accept that as a valid proposition at all and to look at the problem in a different way.

Undisputed Territory

Of the three types of need shown in the model, the real bone of contention in organizations is the area labeled "overlap." Both the organization as an identifiable entity and the people within that organization feel a sense of ownership of the items that fall within the middle ground of the model.

In general, the other two areas are undisputed territory. Management feels most strongly about the well-being of the organization. The average person who is part of the organization cares, but his concern is much less intense. Similarly, management feels much less concern about the items listed as "people needs," while the average worker regards them as the key issues in the business.

As an example, take the matter of adequate wages. Despite the headlines this issue gets, it's not really a matter for violent disagreement in most organizations. The disagreements are disagreements of degree—a few cents an hour or a few dollars a month. Both parties recognize that only so much is possible and agree pretty well on the definition of "adequate."

Similarly, there is very little disagreement about the need for personal recognition or for job security or for individual growth. The perspective of organization management and of the people subject to that management may be different, but both admit to the need and try to attend to it.

As regards the overall needs of the organization, the individual employee normally feels that balancing the disparate interests of himself, the customer, and the shareholder is a management problem. In fact he has only a dim perception that this is a problem. Many businessmen deeply regret the worker's isolationism on this issue, and one of the perennial information campaigns in business is an attempt to educate workers to share management's concern about the economic realities of the business.

But most of these campaigns are dismal failures because the issues are too far removed from the worker's experience. And even when the worker feels the impact of customer disinterest or rejection and loses his job, he tends to blame management for not doing its job. In his view the customer is simply not his problem. The obvious exceptions to this are the employees who have substantial customer contact, but rarely are they able to transmit their experience or concern to the interior of the organization.

Similarly, any demands made by society or government on the business also tend to draw a collective shrug of the shoulder from nonmanagement people. And productivity usually is perceived as a matter of "their wanting me to work harder so they can make more money."

My point is that there seems to be a number of significant issues which both management and the labor force have reserved mainly as their own. Ironically, they both have given tacit recognition to each other's ownership of these problems, a fact that is lamented by a good many neutral observers. But perhaps there is enough mutual understanding of the issues so that this division is not the problem it is sometimes claimed to be by those who would like to see shared perceptions and shared responsibility on every matter facing the organization.

Some Unresolved Questions

The middle, or overlap, area of the model is a different proposition. And that area, in my judgment, is to a large extent the source of the fallacy that attending to people and their concerns is done at the expense of efficiency and results.

Except for profit and growth, four of the five factors listed in that middle part are related to the individual's work experience. In other words, these factors have a profound influence on his day-to-day life on the job. Because the world of work is such an important part of the life and identity of contemporary Americans, it is hard to exaggerate the impact of those factors on the very quality of modern life.

Needless to say, because these issues matter there is substantial—though not necessarily visible or audible —disagreement on each factor. What, for example, constitutes job mastery? The individual has a deep need to feel that he's mastered his work. In the beginning of any new job, that need is all-absorbing of the worker's attention and it often produces a good deal of anxiety. For its part, the organization also needs competent people. But what is job mastery in objective terms? Is it producing so many units per hour? Is it meeting a set of objectives which have been delivered from on high?

167

Is it a feeling of oneness and of general satisfaction with one's labor? Is it a sense of personal worth and accomplishment?

Those who primarily value the end product and those who primarily value people are locked in fundamental disagreement on such an issue. And similarly, we can dissect each of the other factors in the middle ground of the model. How much profit and growth? And out of whose hide or at what cost to the well-being of the organization? And, similarly, to what purpose and according to whose priorities should order be kept and planning carried out?

How much predictability will people be permitted? At what point, for example, does disclosure of the worsening state of the business begin to damage the organization's reputation? Will people be told the truth about the business so they can plan their own careers? These are all real and important questions, and there is significant disagreement as to how they should be resolved.

And, of course, the issue of meaningful work is one of very long standing. What drives the process of job design? Will it be human needs or will those needs be outweighed by the needs of the organization for higher productivity and greater efficiency?

None of these questions has been resolved at this point, and they will be the subject of increasing debate in years to come as we switch from labor-intensive work to so-called knowledge work. Interestingly, they also constitute the arena in which the battle over human needs versus technological and organizational needs will be fought.

The Reward-Punishment Technique

In general, those who see the human resource as merely a part of the production equation support the reward-punishment technique of managing people. If people achieve goals and objectives in some measurable fashion, they are to be rewarded. Conversely, if they fail to meet these same goals and objectives, they must be punished in some visible and meaningful way and made example of. The equation is so objective and so simple that it has great appeal to the tough-minded managers of the world.

And from there we need not go very far to reach the conclusion that any failure to punish people is permissive management that can only lead to more failure. Nor need we go far to reach the conclusion that if a manager pays too much attention to human needs, he does so at the expense of production and efficiency.

What all of this ignores is that the changing nature of work from manual to intellectual labor is imposing a new set of demands on people. The reward-punishment style of management tends to produce people who are adept at keeping a low profile, who refuse to take the risks that are an inherent part of innovation and of creative contribution.

What we apparently need to learn is how to manage people in such a way that they will accept responsibility, take appropriate risks, and approach the job with imagination and dedication. I seriously question if those kinds of behavior are encouraged by simple reward and punishment responses from management.

169

Rather than manipulate people in this fashion, we must learn what kind of work environment they really thrive in. We must also discover the kinds of rewards that motivate them to give their best to the organization. What we must stop is the *mindless* punishment and the *mindless* reward of our human resources.

In fact I would go so far as saying that we should eliminate punishment altogether as a way of dealing with organizational mistakes. Punishment does not correct anything or anyone in a work environment. It serves only to engender resentment and the desire for retribution, which, in the long run, the victim will succeed in exacting from the organization. In my judgment the real solution to many of these problems lies in the manner in which we reward people.

Drawbacks of the Reward System

The existing reward system in organizations tends to do at least four wrong things. It encourages people:

To seek management positions whether or not they really want them or are suited for them. The greatest material rewards are in management, so most people are encouraged and expected to aspire to management positions.

To politick for personal promotion. This second effect of the reward system is largely a product of the first. Recognition and visibility are important to anyone who desires to be promoted. That means that ownership of an idea becomes more important than the idea itself.

To put personal goals ahead of the well-being of the organization as a whole. Again this phenomenon is a function of the reward system. Promotion is an individual end which is often pursued with little regard for the good of the organization. Political infighting and territorial squabbles are often seen as more significant than what's best for the company.

To seek ways to add additional layers or departments to the organization. Managers can't be created or promoted unless there are something and someone for them to manage. Thus the organization is sometimes artificially organized and divided to suit this "need."

Clearly, a more sensible reward system would save its greatest rewards for those who *move* the organization toward its goals of productivity and customer responsiveness. It would reward real creativity and effective planning. And it certainly would address itself to the task of making managers of only those people with the qualifications and the desire to manage.

Employee Participation in Planning?

Obviously, some company reward systems are better than others in meeting those needs. Some are utterly inadequate. The point of this discussion is that the real task in a vital, living organization is to keep the organization in motion toward its goals in such a way that the employee is able to contribute as fully and as imaginatively as he can. In today's world I believe that means that he may well be a much more active participant in planning as well as doing his work.

171

A communications colleague of mine, Myron (Mike) Emanuel of DuPont, calls this the phenomenon of "I want in," or of "codetermination." I don't believe that, in the 1970s, there is any successful way to exclude people from at least some degree of such codetermination. Further, it would seem to be in the long-term best interests of any business to tap as much of its people's talents and energies as possible. Participative management, in which the employee is a party to planning and goal-setting, seems to be one of the best ways to do that.

This does not mean that every unit of every organization must turn itself into a corporate democracy. The hard truth is that some of the people who want codetermination are incapable of participating in the business. They simply do not have the understanding, the talent, or the perspective to do so. Many of the studies of participative management point to the logical conclusion that, in order to participate in any process, the employee must be experienced, informed, and interested. At that point, he or she is ready to contribute some meaningful advice or to make worthwhile suggestions.

That requirement should be perfectly obvious, but it's amazing how often managers who should know better seem to believe that participative management is inherently superior to any other management style—mostly, I suppose, because it seems to be more democratic. They ignore the simple fact that the composition of the work group—the talent or lack of it among its members, their commitment or lack of it, their own aspirations and their relationships with one another—

172

tends to dictate how the manager will be able to manage and what management style matches the situation.

Peter Drucker, in fact, suggests that participative management tends to be beyond the capabilities of many humans.[1] He cites particularly the weak, the vulnerable, and the damaged, who can't handle the responsibility and the self-discipline which are required. The question the manager needs to ask, says Drucker, is, "What is the reality of *my* situation and how can I discharge *my* task of managing workers and working in today's situation?"

Enlarging the Areas of Overlap

The premise that we must be *either* people-oriented *or* results-oriented is a phony issue. These concerns are not in opposition to one another. The first requirement for beginning to humanize any organization is to manage it in such a way that its systems and procedures are suited to enlarging the area of correspondence between people needs and organization needs. As those areas come closer together, the organization becomes by definition a much more habitable human environment.

That task of enlarging the real areas of overlap is really the task we all must share if we are to make our work lives mean anything to us and to our society. If we do it well, I believe the bottom line will largely take care of itself. If we fail, I suspect that we will also fail as profit-making institutions.

Ultimately, the successful work relationship must be based on mutual respect and mutual concern, and on the recognition and satisfaction of mutual needs. When that fact is as widely recognized and accepted as the traditional belief that there is unending conflict between business needs and people needs, the task of humanizing will be well under way.

Dr. Robert Pearse, a professor of behavioral science at the Boston University School of Management, says that there is a shift away from the "people-using" organization and toward the "people-building" organization.[2] He points out that in the two older organizational models—the entrepreneurial and the bureaucratic—people were used. In the entrepreneurial organization, they were seen as mere instruments of production, as human machines. In Pearse's words, the choice was "produce or perish."

In bureaucracies, it is the low-profile manager who succeeds. He is sensitive to the power shifts above him and thrives on inertia and conformity. Both of these forms, Pearse says, are headed for trouble: "The truly professionally managed organization is people conscious —people are central rather than merely peripheral to organizational planning and development." He asserts further that people-building organizations are going to fare better in the future than those which continue to ignore the very special resources that only human beings bring to the organization.

Developing and managing those resources to deal with the complex social and economic environment of the future may well be the key to both corporate profit and the general well-being of our society in the years ahead.

The People Builders

In a world in which change is the one constant, we will certainly have to train people to be both flexible and resourceful. Alvin Toffler suggests that most people see bureaucracy as one of the major threats to our society in the years ahead. He discounts that concern simply because an inflexible organization or system will not be able to cope with the accelerating rate of change we are experiencing.

Within our business organizations I see encouraging signs that people are beginning to understand that the only way to create flexible and innovative organizations is to design systems which *develop* people rather than *use* them. That may sound like a simple and ridiculously obvious thing to do, but in most of our organizations it will mean radical, if not revolutionary, change.

Prisonlike Environments

Traditionally, our organizations have laid a heavy hand on their people. The emphasis was on creating a disciplined work force which took its direction and its policies from on high. People were encouraged to seek authorizations for any but routine decisions and actions. The clear signal was, When in doubt, check and double-check. In this kind of environment, people became expert at sharing responsibility and covering all their tracks so that the path of any mistake could not possibly be traced back to their doorsteps.

The external signs of such an organization can be

175

easily read. In the factory there are bells and whistles to signal when work begins and ends and when breaks are allowed. There are foremen patrolling the aisles to see that everyone is busy—or at least looks busy. In fact, the whole thing is depressingly like the Edward G. Robinson prison-laundry scenes in which the doors clang shut on the convicts for the work day. The stampede of people out the doors of such factories to the parking lot at night is a pretty good indicator of how they feel about the place.

On the office side, things are generally a little more human—but not much. I recall one office I was in some years ago where the management decided that coffee breaks had got out of hand. Their solution was to program everyone for a 15-minute break, morning and afternoon, in the company cafeteria. The predictable result was that people who had not taken a coffee break before now found it to be an essential part of their schedule. Worse yet, most people took 30 minutes rather than 15, and the company wound up losing, rather than gaining, work time.

In such an environment the manager is normally subject to so many checks and balances that he correctly sees himself as a straw boss rather than a leader. The people he "manages" are like all of the other company resources he has been given. They represent a certain cost factor which must be amortized against the product as "labor costs." Little or no thought is given to their ability to innovate, to create, or to care about their work.

176

The Bureaucratic Nerve Center

Generally, the personnel function in such an organization becomes the nerve center of the bureaucracy. It defines itself as the inventor and the enforcer of the system. Any employee who seeks protection against the inflexibilities of the system or who looks to the personnel people for help discovers very quickly that he has squealed on the SS to the Gestapo. He regrets his new visibility and his identification as a troublemaker.

What I am sketching is exaggerated, but I know a few organizations where it's not overstated by very much. In fact, the personnel organization and its attitudes are very often the best barometer of an organization's real atmosphere. If they are oppressive, the organization surely will be oppressive. If they are enlightened, it's a good bet that the organization as a whole will be enlightened.

In the oppressive, people-using companies, the personnel people very often function as surrogate line managers. By that, I mean that they are expected to do the manager's people tasks directly. He is left to meeting deadlines and holding the line on costs, but he is not expected to develop or counsel his people except to plan their work, to give them their orders for the day, and, of course, to supervise them closely.

A New Role for Managers

In the enlightened companies I know about, I see this mode of operation being abandoned as fast as management can do it. In these organizations, the personnel function becomes a resource and a counseling function for the manager in meeting his clearly stated people responsibilities. *The manager* is the one who must help people formulate their individual career plans, the one who must counsel them about their job performance and what they must do to become more proficient and more effective, the one who must be available when they need advice and attention.

For most managers who have been managing for a few years, this is a role they don't understand very well. Some, in fact, would even deny its legitimacy. But this role is certainly in keeping with some of the changing public views toward authority and the primacy of the individual.

The manager is particularly vulnerable in the whole area of government Affirmative Action policy, because the company can be held responsible for his misdeeds, his bias, or his ignorance of Affirmative Action demands. That practical fact plus the ideological changes outlined in Chapter 1 are drastically altering the manner in which managements are dealing with their people problems. They are especially altering the role of personnel people from that of enforcers to that of ombudsmen for the work force.

All of these changes should be welcomed by the people who are truly interested in managing people instead of systems. What they mean is greater flexibility and greater freedom in getting the job done.

Of course, they also mean greater responsibility for the manager, because he or she must be sensitive to people's needs and prepared to provide honest feedback about their performance and their shortcomings. That is not an easy task, and it usually is not a very pleasant one. It can and does strain manager-subordinate relationships. Much depends on the nature of that relationship in the first place. If it's honest and built on mutual trust and mutual respect, then it is not going to be destroyed by candor.

The insecure manager, like the insecure parent, is often afraid to deal honestly and openly with subordinates. Instead, he or she retreats to authority and prerogatives and denies people the constructive criticism they need for corrective action and for personal growth.

The manager is also under added responsibility in identifying his own failings and correcting them with suitable self-development programs. This emphasis on tailor-made self-development is an interesting trend documented by Pearse in his AMA study on management development.

It is Pearse, incidentally, who argues for a more complete approach to human resources development for manager training.[3] He cites an important shift in what he calls the "lifeline" of an organization. He notes that in the future, organizational survival and growth will depend on effective employment and development of human resources because such measures will make the difference in coping with high technology demands and with rapid change.

Pearse says this is in contrast to the traditional lifeline of the past, which was effective production and marketing. These were the old keys to survival. In the future, people-building will thus become a critical task for the business organization.

Further, Pearse points out, there is a growing body of knowledge about professional management that can be systematically taught to the new manager. Presumably, this knowledge can help make him more effective on the job. Add to that the fact that demands and pressures will encourage him more and more to develop his own skills and it seems safe to presume that people-building behavior will be much more manifest in our organizations in the months and years ahead than it has been in the past.

Conflicting Goals

On a related matter, behavioral scientist Chris Argyris takes the position that the goals of the traditional organization (the people-using organization) and the goals and needs of the individual are in serious conflict as we are now operating.[4] Organizations, according to his model, have tended to strive to control individual behavior by designing specialized and fractionalized work, by controlling the speed of work, by giving orders, by evaluating performance, and by rewarding and punishing.

He asserts, on the other hand, that people in general try to achieve relative independence and autonomy, that they strive to develop many abilities and to become proficient in a few, and that they seek to develop a time perspective that is longer than a work cycle—that, in fact, focuses on the long haul.

In brief, the organization is often, through its jobs, controls, and leadership, trying to *reduce* individual autonomy (i.e., to *use* people) at the same time that people are trying to establish their independence and to build their maturity. The result of this conflict for the individual—who must subordinate his needs to those of the organization—is frustration.

When he is thus frustrated, the employee reacts either by fighting the organization, leaving it temporarily or permanently, becoming apathetic toward it, or by substituting money as a reward for meaningless work. Obviously, all four of these responses are more or less detrimental to both the organization and the individual.

How one views this rather depressing conflict of goals depends on one's conception of man and of the status quo. Some observers have looked at these kinds of models and have concluded that we must forget about self-actualization. They assert we must go beyond the concepts of freedom and dignity to teach people to live within the corporate world *as it is,* to adjust to external authority of this kind.

I believe with Argyris that that conclusion is dead wrong.

The task is to begin to explore the more difficult challenge of how to encourage and permit individuals to be responsible adults and to behave as whole human beings in moving their organizations toward worthwhile goals.

Organizations which are not prepared to face the responsibility of building people and providing a work environment that meets the human need for purpose and satisfaction are simply not prepared to meet the challenge of managing adults. That challenge is one of the major tasks which face us now and will face us in the future. Of necessity, it will require a different people perspective for corporate management in general. Some of the other new perspectives they must cope with are explored in the next section.

The Need for New Perspectives

Businessmen, perhaps more than most other institutional managers, are highly susceptible to slogans. Those which deal with the sanctity of free enterprise, competition, increased productivity, growth, and government interference have always been particularly popular.

The trouble with these slogans is precisely that they *are* slogans. It is difficult to challenge most of them because they sound like a sacred litany of business rights. Actually, they are more like a form of business-speak in which one ends an argument by invoking a slogan which one's opponent is, by definition, not allowed to question.

The worst part of such discourse is that it prohibits any intelligent debate about business goals and business values at a time when such debate is badly needed. The givens of nineteenth- and twentieth-century economic theory become the givens of the present and the future. It is hard to imagine a more sterile perspective in an age when the world is beset with unprecedented problems of inflation, energy shortages, food shortages, and over-population, to cite just a few.

Education or Propaganda?

This particular problem of business-speak was brought home to me dramatically at a national communications meeting on economic issues. The purpose of the meeting was to determine how business could do a better job of informing employees and the public about profit, productivity, and the like. It was a gathering of some of the most talented industrial communications people in the country—and a rather depressing experience, because much of the program and the sample handouts were sheer sloganeering.

Haverford College President John Coleman took the group to task for not knowing whether it wanted to educate or to propagandize. His well-taken point was simply that economic issues are terribly complex and to present them in simplistic terms was a disservice to both the public and to the institutions we were representing.

He was especially distressed with the ploy of making government the adversary of business in so many of the "educational" materials on display. His was one of the few discordant voices at the conference as most of the other speakers pointed with evident pride and self-congratulation to the morality tales published by their respective organizations as an answer to both potential and actual criticism of their operations.

In one of the more comic moments of the conference, one company executive actually noted that the

183

productivity campaign he had on display was not really intended to increase productivity. When pressed for some information about its measurable impact on employee productivity, he replied that it really was an "image-building" campaign. That remark should have been greeted with hoots of derisive laughter, but nobody wanted to rub his nose in the obvious fact that he was doing his job as he had been instructed to do it.

No Corporation Is an Island

Somehow the top management of that company, and thought-leaders in business in general, must break out of these stereotypes that dominate their thinking about business and begin to think more critically about their role in the real world. They will never accomplish that until they begin to look past appearances to the realities of the business corporation and their own individual roles in our modern world.

Clearly, the interdependence of that world does not permit anyone to carry on this role in isolation, to think that his survival is his own affair and that the rest of humanity's survival is their affair. This is true of individuals, it is true of institutions, and it is certainly true of nations.

Author Sir Geoffrey Vickers has expressed his concern about the isolation of those organizations which interlock their interests so closely that they generate their own standards of success and virtually escape from the control of the people who should be controlling them.[5] Such organizations, he says, behave like a cancerous growth with no purpose but to live and grow.

His vision of the future, in England at least, is of a further shift of resources from individual to collective use. Along with that he sees a growth in government power to ensure that institutions and organizations are responsive to the general welfare of the people.

His views would likely evoke a knee-jerk reaction of alarm and dismay from most of the sloganeering businessmen I spoke of earlier. But the facts of life are such that the proper role of the businessman today is twofold: to be certain that his enterprise is as successful as it can be (because that is basic to everything else), and to be certain that it operates responsibly and honorably in a world which is in great need of responsible leadership and stewardship.

A Bankrupt View of Capitalism

Some businessmen looking back on the values and goals of the old technocracy, with its emphasis on efficiency and technology, would claim that this two-fold role is contradictory. They argue from the nineteenth-century perspective of laissez faire economic doctrine that blind profit-seeking is finally in the public good, that the invisible hand of capitalism converts private vices into public benefits.

Such diverse thinkers as economist John Kenneth Galbraith, sociologist Daniel Bell of Harvard, and management expert Peter Drucker all see this as a bankrupt view of modern capitalism. Each in his own way calls on business managers to manifest a sense of public responsibility in their decision-making and their planning.

Galbraith argues for a new socialism in which the traditionally weak but important industries would be organized under public ownership.[6] He has in mind particularly: housing, the health industry, and transportation, because of their public significance and traditionally inequitable distribution systems. He also proposes as a rule of thumb that all companies which do more than half their business with the government be converted into fully public corporations.

Bell takes a slightly less drastic line than Galbraith, seeing government as the "cockpit" of the future.[7] In tracing for us the evolution of the corporation in America along an imaginary continuum, he identifies at one extreme what he calls the "economizing mode," in which all aspects of organization are single-mindedly directed to profit and growth. At the other extreme is the "sociologizing mode," in which all workers have a lifetime job and the satisfaction of their needs becomes the primary tax on resources.

Bell asserts that in the last 30 years the corporation has been moving steadily toward the sociologizing mode. Coupled with the corporation's heightened awareness of its social responsibilities to various elements of society, that leads Bell to the conclusion that ". . . we in America are moving away from a society based on a private-enterprise market system toward one in which the most important economic decisions will be made at the political level, in terms of consciously defined 'goals' and 'priorities.' " His position, like Galbraith's, is that the free-enterprise society no longer satisfies the citizenry, so it will have to be changed in some yet-to-be-defined way to make it more responsive to public needs.

Drucker takes vehement exception to Galbraith's call for a new socialism, saying that such monolithic structures are "wasteful, rigid, and stifling." [8] Instead, he insists that corporate managements must be autonomous and private because this autonomy is in the long-run best interests of society.

However, he issues a strong caveat along with his call for management autonomy. He warns the contemporary manager of the need to be public in outlook and to accept the *moral* responsibility and the *moral* principle of organization. That responsibility, which is to be the manager's imperative, is to make individual strengths productive in achieving social benefits. Drucker insists that the manager must make work productive and the worker an achiever, and he must help improve the overall quality of our lives.

Despite their differences about means, all three men arrive at the same basic conclusion: *The business corporation derives its right to operate from its ability to serve mankind.* When it loses this ability or when it turns its back on this responsibility, it displays a degree of arrogance which calls into question its very right to survive.

Facing the Real Responsibilities

That issue with all of its implications is the one we will have to address in determining what kind of business organizations we will build and sustain in the future. The ensuing debate on that matter must be carried on without rancor and without blind commitment to the values of the older technocracy. Neither new slogans nor old ones will serve us in this vital discussion.

Some observers have objected and will continue to object that such matters are not the concern of corporate enterprise and if they are made their concern, the basic mission of profit and growth will be undermined. That really is no longer the point, if it ever was. If corporate managements do not make a conscious effort to understand these issues and to come to grips with them in today's world, they may well find themselves facing a progressively angrier and more hostile public until finally their organizations are refashioned without their counsel or their consent.

Toffler has detailed the consequences of uncontrolled change and the chaos it has unleashed on all of us; one of his clear admonitions for the future is the need for careful and informed planning.[9] No longer do we have the luxury of claiming that the consequences are not really our concern, whether we are speaking of the total society or of the actions of one organization.

Here is a handful of the long-term consequences of uncontrolled growth and change in the U.S. alone:

The destruction of the family-unit rural economy.

The centralization of industrial wealth (87 of the *Fortune* 500 companies own 46 percent of our total manufacturing assets).

The consequent dependence of the individual on an

industrial system geared to its own perpetuation and often indifferent to his personal welfare.

A nomadic life-style in which thousands of families pack up and move from city to city every three or four years in pursuit of "corporate success."

Migration to the urban ghettos of the north by poor blacks expelled from the land by agricultural mechanization and centralization.

In some degree, the advent of the nuclear family without room or patience for elderly parents or other family members, and so forth through a seemingly endless list.

It is tempting to ask how many of us who are so profoundly affected by all of this would have chosen it consciously if that choice had been available to us.

That has to be one of the all-time academic questions because nobody ever did ask us. In fact, in the economizing mode our opinion was regarded as simply irrelevant—so long as we were "good" consumers and "good" workers.

The real question today is the kind of world we want to live in and our right to decide that. We simply cannot leave that question to be resolved by happenstance as has been our tradition. It must be addressed consciously, diligently, and continuously by institutional managements who acknowledge the responsibility that accompanies their great power.

If our corporate institutions are among the most powerful agencies in our society, then they must voluntarily help to restore our lives and our spirits to our own hands. That, of course, by definition means that they must recognize their new role in the larger society and react to changing values and attitudes in an intelligent and responsible way. In the process they must also accept and assume a leadership role in the society.

Forging the New Corporate Dogma

So here we are in the midst of a deep and compelling struggle with our beliefs, our values, our crises, and our individual and collective needs. That struggle probably could not have come at a worse time because, on top of everything else, we have shed many of the standards and the absolutes with which we used to measure such problems. It could be argued with some merit that some of those absolutes served us imperfectly and that they were not totally accurate measures, but at least they were measures of some kind.

The point is that if we reject what we regard as the fallacies of the past, we must replace them with something we *can* believe in. Man is not psychologically equipped for nihilism. He lives to be for some things and against others. Without that opportunity and without the ability to make normative judgments, he has no sense of purpose in his life. And without purpose, life becomes pointless and depressing.

It is beyond the scope of this book, and of my limited powers, to prophesy what will finally come of any collective efforts to make our organizations more human.

190

But I remain convinced that that task is the essential one if we are going to live productive lives within our organizations and within a free society. That task is the one which can give us the sense of meaning we now need so badly.

Powerless people rarely feel good about their lives and their prospects. And this is perhaps the basic issue we face. Are we going to sit by while events do us in? Or are we going to try to regain some sense of mastery over events and over our lives?

I would hazard the opinion that feelings of powerlessness are the basic concern now frustrating so many Americans. They see economic deterioration. They see political deterioration. They see breakdowns in traditional social and moral systems. And they see serious deficiencies in institutional leadership. And worst of all, they have come to believe that there is little or nothing they can do about it all.

Corporate Responsibilities

When Drucker raises the issue of organizational legitimacy, I believe he is on exactly the right track. His conclusion in *Management: Tasks, Responsibilities, Practices* is: "It is the task of *this* management generation to make the institutions of the society . . . perform for society and economy; for the community; and for the individual alike." [10]

If any organization neglects to live up to these collective responsibilities, it surely must be marked down

191

as a failure—regardless of how successful it is on the scales of economic measures. The self-centered organization which operates without regard for any interests beyond those its leadership defines as its own special interests will finally be seen as corrupt.

The company which makes and sells shoddy products, which treats its people as throwaway items who can be confined to a human scrap heap at will, which is oblivious to the needs and concerns of the have-nots of the world, which arrogantly buys and sells any politicians who happen to be for hire, and which operates generally in a manner counter to the public good will be hard pressed to justify its existence in the years ahead. We can no more tolerate such corporate irresponsibility than we can tolerate political chicanery or unethical and corrupt public officials.

We are entering an era where corporations will be subject to greater public scrutiny than they have ever known, where the public may well insist that they establish their very right to exist.

This will be especially so if some of the large and powerful special interests in our country—whether they be business institutions, labor unions, the lobbyists who manipulate their favorite congressmen, or whatever interest group—continue to disregard the larger interest of the nation.

Here in the mid-1970s in the grips of a painful recession, we find ourselves largely unable to deal with events because no one seems willing or able to provide serious and effective leadership which will demand sacrifices in the name of the public good. If that unwillingness or inability continues, it will surely lead to further paralysis, chaos, and wholesale suffering within the republic in the years to come.

A Series of Confrontations

I prefer to believe that somehow we will come to our senses and finally do what has to be done. In this regard Daniel Bell has an interesting construct of man's history.[11] He sees it in terms of confrontations. Man's first confrontation was with nature and his need to forge his survival in the face of nature's vicissitudes. After thousands of years of this struggle, his second confrontation was with technology and his need to make things so that he could rework nature, so that he could increase his human power and replace the natural order. This was the Industrial Revolution.

The third confrontation, which Bell terms "post-industrial society," is concerned primarily with human relationships, with the social world. In the first confrontation the primary reality experienced by man was nature. In the second it was material objects. In the new confrontation it becomes people. The task now is to build a social order in which the possibilities of human freedom and human development are our major concerns.

Given the corruptibility of human nature and the tension between our desire to build and our desire to destroy and do violence, this is an awesome confrontation. And without a clear set of normative concepts to guide us, it is also a very bewildering confrontation.

193

The Need for a New Self-Image

In a word, we need a sense of the ideal. We need a vision to guide us in trying to form ourselves and our society. Archibald MacLeish once said, "The soul of a people is the image it cherishes of itself; the aspect in which it sees itself against the past; the attributes to which its future conduct must respond. To destroy that image is to destroy . . . the identity of a nation." [12]

In the aftermath of the single-mindedness of the Cold War, the senselessness and the suffering of Vietnam, and the arrogant challenge to constitutional government of Watergate, the image is badly in need of restoration. Somehow we must join our efforts in restating and reaffirming that image as a guide to the work we must do in creating a suitable and habitable post-industrial society.

For the business organization that means a new corporate dogma to replace the old. It means the agony of developing and applying new ideals, new values. More specifically, it means intensified effort by corporate leaders to be more sensitive to human needs, it means considerably more effective planning both domestically and internationally, it means a reorientation particularly of the management style and techniques of middle and first-line managers, it means renewed dedication on the part of all of us to work within our large organizations to make them serve us rather than dominate us, and it means managing our organizations in such a way that they earn the right to public respect and support.

194

The Problem of Folklore

All of these things obviously represent radical departures from present practice. Some would say their attainment would represent a minor miracle since the organizations which most of us know on an intimate day-to-day basis simply don't exemplify those characteristics. Certainly the folklore which permeates most of those organizations tells people that there is a world of difference between this ideal and what they see as the real world.

In the average business organization, the folklore says: "Look, the only thing that counts is results. Get them any way you can. And remember that if you don't get them, you will be put out on the street. Human needs are insignificant and can be considered only *after* the results have been obtained. If there's time and energy left over, then we'll attend to other things. In the meantime, just do your job."

The folklore similarly gives short shrift to planning efforts:

"That planning business is a good exercise, but we all know that when the going gets tough, the plans are shelved. At that point the only thing that counts is tomorrow and the weeks ahead. So forget that planning crap."

On the matter of encouraging and rewarding those who are socially and humanly oriented, the folklore is equally plain spoken: "The real job is to produce and cover your ass. Nice guys finish last, so if you're smart,

195

you'll just take care of old number one. That's a jungle out there, and don't ever forget it."

And, finally, on the issue of productivity, the folklore also has preached a different homily: "The way to get things done is to reward and punish. If they do the work the way you want it done, reward them. If not, punish them. Keep the pressure on, or they'll dog it."

Whatever the experts have told us about motivation and why and how people work, the folklore has tended to dominate our day-to-day practices—so much so that those who have proposed changes in our approach to these matters have usually been attacked as empty-headed idealists. Over and over again, when they have wanted to try this or that plan or program, permission has been given with the grim admonition of "OK, OK, but this had better work."

The rest of that line, of course, was implied rather than stated. But it was clearly a situation like the old Rumpelstiltskin tale in which the maiden was always given a single evening to spin her straw into gold—or be executed in the morning.

How Businesses Used to Succeed

It would be instructive to ask why this has normally been so. Is it because we are basically so pragmatic that we can look only at the yield of a given process or program? Is it because we have been willing to throw people bodily into the production hopper and see their labor as only another cost? Is it because we've been addicted to social Darwinism and the belief that life is a struggle in which the strongest are the ones who deserve to survive?

It's partly those things, but it has more to do with the skills which have traditionally enabled a business to succeed. Throughout most of the Industrial Revolution, it was necessary to do two things: You had to build the better mousetrap, and you had to know how to entice the world to beat a path to your door. In short, you had to be an efficient producer, and at the same time you had to understand the sales and marketing process and perform it well.

Most companies that did those two things well could count on surviving and growing. The game was not all that difficult to understand. You kept your costs as low as possible, and you sold the product at a price the customer was willing to pay. In that equation, people were simply another cost. And if they were a cost, the task was to derive as much return as possible from that cost. In the early days of the Industrial Revolution that led to pure and simple exploitation of human labor.

While outright exploitation eventually became close to impossible to carry off, in the United States at least, some of the old attitudes about people still linger on. And, in fact, many organizations even in the 1970s are essentially people-using organizations.

The Ground Rules Are Changing

However as we shift from labor-intensive kinds of work, largely through automation, to work with a smaller content of manual labor, the ground rules of the game change. The so-called knowledge worker—the person who survives in an organization by selling his or her knowledge rather than physical strength or labor—puts a new perspective on the problem.

In our interconnected socioeconomic environment, production and sales, while important, are no longer the key to business survival. That key, most business thinkers agree, is the ability to forecast events and needs and to plan the business strategy so that the corporation is ready to meet emerging needs. In turn that demands planned innovation and the efficient use of human resources. To return to an earlier figure of speech, today you must be preparing to build the mousetrap with only an imperfect idea of what a mouse even is.

In that sort of environment the ability to think problems through, to anticipate the effect of all sorts of change, and to liberate people from whatever systems or parts of systems inhibit creative work becomes paramount. It also sets in motion a great tension between those managers who want to operate in the people-using mode and their people, who are struggling not to be so inhibited in their duties and responsibilities that they become ineffectual. Truly, that is an agony for both parties.

The person who can understand human productivity only in so many units per man-hour is tormented by his inability to measure knowledge work in familiar terms. An interesting aside in this question is how such people will function and are functioning in times of economic downturn. Such declines in the business cycle always tempt management to look for hard-and-fast measures of work and to throw overboard any project or person seen as ballast when the ship is foundering.

But the point is that given the accelerating rate of change we have known in recent years and given the obvious requirement that we must improve our ability to anticipate and plan for change, the emerging management environment is very different. It calls not only for new techniques but also for new dogma.

People-using practices were almost always justified by their supporters on economic and survival grounds. If the business was to make it, they argued, there was no choice. This was the way it had to be.

Those who attack the emerging management techniques and the greater individual concern that comes with them usually do so from the people-using perspective that they are "bad for the business." And yet if the likes of Toffler, Drucker, and others are right, then business survival depends on people-building and not on people-using practices.

A New Corporate Dogma

Hence, the need for a new corporate dogma, which can be reduced roughly to the following major points:

Precept number one is that *corporate leadership will succeed in the emerging corporate environment in proportion to its real ability to achieve goals related to the human needs of worker, consumer, and the society at large.* Clearly, an interconnected world does not permit corporate leaders or any other kind of leaders to take an atomistic view of their roles. They must see and re-

199

spect the connections if their businesses are to be seen as legitimate enterprises and indeed if they are to be allowed to operate by the nations and the societies which give them their charters.

The second precept is related to the first. *Corporate actions and policies will have to be planned and implemented with due regard for their impact on the society in which the corporation functions.* Corporate responsibility certainly exceeds the narrow interpretation of community lip service and contribution which that term once signified. What will be required literally is responsibility to and for the society and the reflection of that sense of responsibility in corporate actions.

Here again is an area that some managers will rail against as external interference in their internal affairs. But when a corporation is engaged in any enterprise which has an important effect on the public welfare, can it ever justify its preoccupation with its self-interest and its own needs? I think not.

The third precept of the new dogma is that *those who move the corporation closer to the achievement of both economic and social goals should be singled out for the greatest rewards.* The late Joseph C. Wilson, who led Xerox to the pinnacle of American corporate life in the late fifties and in the sixties used to say, "You have to do well before you can do good." He never forgot that the businessman's first responsibility is to be successful so that the corporation can meet the diverse demands made upon it by society for goods, jobs, services, and social responsiveness.

In general, business has done fairly well in rewarding those who make substantial contributions to the organization's technical and marketing success. That point might be challenged by fair numbers of people who believe their contributions have not been properly recognized, but I believe it to be a fairly sound generalization about American business.

On the issue of rewarding those who have sought to remind the corporation of its social responsibilities, the track record is not anywhere near as good. The problem is that people have been paid traditionally to affect the balance sheet. Social accomplishment to this point has not been measured as a corporate asset or a positive return on investment. In fact, the measures which have been devised are not very satisfactory and not really in general use.

The result is that most corporate people have dabbled in social responsibility as board (and sometimes bored) members of community groups or as volunteers to those organizations they supported. But most of that activity has been seen as an extracurricular burden rather than an integral part of the person's corporate responsibilities.

The challenge is to raise the social consciousness of all business leaders so that they see corporate responsibility not as a subject for TV commercials and four-color ads but as an essential ingredient of business decision-making. Indeed, the inability to recognize the social dimension of business problems and decisions could become the businessman's fatal flaw in the years ahead.

In the aftermath of a 1974 U.N. conference on hunger and world food shortages, the chief executive of a U.S. food-processing company made a speech asserting that a bumper crop would be the worst thing that could happen to U.S. farmers and to his industry because it would drive prices down. The juxtaposition in time of that food congress and of his speech was a dramatic illustration of the point I'm making here. The possibility of developing a delivery system to transfer the surplus to the starving nations had simply been written off as unrealistic.

When I had occasion shortly afterward at a management workshop to raise this issue with a group of middle and first-line managers of a West Coast food packer, they could not understand the point I was making. And, in fact, one of them told me that he had often seen surplus peaches buried to maintain price levels when there was a bumper crop. I mention this episode only to show how far we have to go in changing the thinking of some management.

It seems to me that this problem will only be addressed when the manager clearly understands that his *total* performance will be measured. And that it will be within a system which reacts with revulsion to burying peaches or to any other act of insensitivity to the needs and welfare of the public.

The fourth precept of the emerging corporate dogma is that *the individual who has the fortitude and the insight to do so should work within the corporate system to humanize it and revitalize it.* Traditionally, in business this has been close to the top of the list of thankless jobs. The folklore has taught people to avoid this kind of role and to look out for themselves instead. It seems to me that the disastrous consequences of that sort of behavior should be apparent to all of us by now.

If we believe that management has a responsibility to the organization and to the interests in the society at large, it is not too much to suggest that the individual worker also has that responsibility. The problem is to manage, reward, and treat people in such a way that they will respond to this obligation.

As I've been suggesting throughout this book, that means understanding their needs and dealing with them as human beings. That means that they operate in an environment where they perform a real job, where their work lives are reasonably predictable, and where their efforts are appreciated and recognized. There is plenty of subjective and objective data to show people respond to that kind of environment and want to give their best effort within it.

In my view we will take a long stride toward improving our organizations when we learn how to produce that sort of environment as a typical work experience. For those who demand to know in advance what the return is on investment in good human relations, I offer them the possibility of a committed and creative work force.

On the other side of this issue I believe that it's imperative for those of us who work in a corporate, or any other kind of, organization to recognize the benefits of engagement. Alienation has been a fashionable posture since the sixties in our organizations. "They" won't let me, "they" oppress me, "they" don't give a damn about their people, and on and on.

The trouble with alienation as a way of life is that it's so lonely. In time the alienated worker is not merely discouraged with management and with the organization; he carries his disaffection to everyone around him including his co-workers, his family, and ultimately himself.

If he stops to think about it, he has to realize that he's punishing some innocent people with some very destructive behavior. The opposite of loyalty and commitment is rarely rebellion or flight. It is normally anger and frustration which are internalized or taken out on scapegoats who can't defend themselves. I find it hard to conceive of a more destructive attitude or to offer a better argument for hanging on in the day-to-day task of humanizing.

Which leads indirectly to a final and important point —namely the question of when to face the fact that one's work environment is hopeless. I think we have to acknowledge that there are some organizations which are so affected by organizational hardening of the arteries that they are like disoriented old men unable to cope with change and firmly committed to the past and its preservation. The important job for the individual caught in such an organization is first to recognize the reality of his situation and then to deal with it as best he can.

If he has an alternative, he should obviously leave such an environment for the sake of his health and his sanity. If no such alternative is available—either because of the lack of suitable opportunities or his own limitations and special circumstances—then the best he can do is stay and carve out as satisfying a work life as the environment permits. That is a difficult and sometimes painful experience, but it's not hopeless. It will depend on his resourcefulness and his ability to channel his energies to those activities and outlets where he can find fulfillment.

For years and years, people caught up in unsatisfying and rather hopeless work have made such an adjustment. The demand for job satisfaction, we must recognize, is a relatively recent one, and it's important for us to understand that in some circumstances it simply may not be attainable.

What is always reasonably attainable in any job environment is the opportunity to establish satisfying relationships with people. I remember one particularly bad job environment I worked in several years ago. There was one person in that organization who always managed to shrug off the unpleasantness that distressed the rest of us. I asked him one day how he managed to keep his composure and always to appear so unruffled. His answer has stuck in my mind. He said:

> First, I can't leave this city for family reasons, and this is one of the best companies in town. Second, I like the people I work with and the work I do. Third, my life off the job is where I really get my satisfaction. And, finally it's always seemed to me that the best thing to do was imitate the flowers and to bloom where you're planted.

205

For his kind of circumstance, I couldn't think of a better solution.

So here we are with what we might regard as the emerging corporate dogma which we can boil down about as follows:

- Corporate leadership must pursue goals attuned to the human needs of worker, consumer, and the larger society.
- Actions and policies must be implemented with due regard for their impact on society.
- Those who achieve *both* the economic and social goals of the organization should be singled out for the greatest rewards. Neither set of goals should ever be pursued without regard for the other.
- The individual in any organization has a responsibility to humanize and to renew it as much as he or she can.

A New Role for All

All of that obviously is quite different from the old dogma whose assured declarative tone did not invite challenge. The emphasis in the new dogma is normative, suggesting a new role for all of us in making our organizations function for the common good.

The English pamphleteer Bernard Mandeville suggested 300 years ago that blind and greedy profit-seeking advances the public good through "the invisible hand" of capitalism. Most people have believed this assertion and have tended to act on the premise that their "private vices would make public benefits."

As a *moral* principle it was bankrupt from the beginning, but in an uncomplicated agrarian society it might have seemed valid. Today's world society, however, is anything but that.

It is more akin to a sleek passenger train hurtling at ever increasing velocity through the darkness with all of us on board. We have begun to realize that the speed of the train is excessive as we head into a series of sharp curves over rolling hills. Do we smile nervously at one another and let whatever is going to happen happen? Or do we make our way forward and demand that the engineer stop playing fast and loose with *our* lives? Or might we even take control of the train?

The metaphor requires no further development. The choice of acting or not acting is firmly up to us as we look at the problem of organizational and institutional rehabilitation.

The burden implicit in all of this will not be easy for those of us who choose to carry it. But in the last 50 years every developed country in the world has arrived at the point where its primary functions are largely entrusted to big organizations. The performance of these organizations increasingly will be the performance of these societies and of our entire planet.

The search for a corporate soul will be one of the most exciting and the most vital tasks of our post-industrial society. It must begin now. And it must begin with each of us by himself or herself. Alone in the beginning, but eventually joined by like-minded people who see the necessity and who are willing to accept the challenge. The critical question is whether or not enough of us will rise to the occasion.

Throughout American economic history we have lived by the now seemingly outmoded values of materialism, individual competition, waste, and the pursuit of industrial and economic growth for its own sake and its own gain. Our changing world is signaling from all sides that we must change this long-standing behavior.

Whether or not we choose to do so will profoundly affect the rest of our lives as well as those of our children and our children's children.

Epilogue: Conclusion

PERSPECTIVE is an elusive but a necessary quality.

There is a feeling in the world today that time is running out on us: We are in the throes of continuing inflation. There is a serious energy shortage which threatens our industrial process and technology in general. We have serious population problems and serious pollution problems. It is also clear that industrial growth as we have known it cannot continue indefinitely. When that growth slows down, there will obviously be problems within and among nations in sharing the world's resources.

All of these are difficult problems which have made us question our ability to deal with them, as well as the ability of our leaders to bring us unscathed into the future. In the face of all of this we seem to be lacking in self-confidence, and our collective morale is none too good. A better sense of human history might help us cope more effectively with both the present and the future.

It has been estimated that if it had been possible to keep a diary of the world from its creation to the present, with only one page for every thousand years, the resulting volumes by now would fill 2 miles of book shelf! In one of these mythical and rather recent volumes (about 500,000 years ago) we would discover the birth of a new creature with the unique capacity to be conscious of his own existence and his own actions. That one creature has changed the face of the earth.[1]

He has cleared forests and jungles, explored and studied his environment on earth, and even traveled to a neighboring planet. He has learned to fashion the tools he needed to conquer and even to control nature. He has built, destroyed, and rebuilt entire civilizations. In one of his more masterful accomplishments, he has learned to organize both work and his fellow humans in such a way that they would actually sacrifice for a purpose they regarded as larger than themselves.

Ironically, in that last accomplishment, he has also had to come to grips with one of his most serious limitations as a creature. His very consciousness of his own self-interest has tended throughout his history to make him self-centered. For at least the past 6000 years in the Judaeo-Christian tradition that has so powerfully influenced his experience, he has been aware of this inner struggle and has sought with varying degrees of success, failure, and guilt to deal with it.

But, once again, to keep things in perspective, we must recognize that of the 500 pages that chronicle man's history on our imaginary bookshelf, only the last six pages tell of this particular struggle. And the subject of human organizations and man's relationship to those organizations is a mere paragraph or two at the bottom of the current page.

As recent and as limited a problem as it may be in the total perspective of human history, it is nonetheless an important one to the future prospects of mankind. If the sharing of scarce resources and concern for those around us are going to be important to our collective survival and to our existence, then we will have to learn compassion and generosity. Such a conversion from self-centered to other-centered behavior will be a radical change in human life and in human priorities. It will take time. It will undoubtedly be painful, but it is finally an ideal we must pursue and achieve if we are not going to go the way of other creatures in history who could not cope with the changing needs of their existence and their environment.

Certainly we will fail in our confrontation with each other (the confrontation that Daniel Bell says will typify postindustrial society) unless we can learn to rise above preoccupation with self and with insulating that self from the rest of the world.

The problem, in American culture at least, is that the solution to the real and potential dehumanization imposed by big, impersonal organizations is often seen to be *disengagement* and *greater* self-preoccupation. Such a "solution" will worsen rather than correct the

211

problem. Such a solution will leave the big and complex organization a freer and freer hand in taking over more of our lives and our freedoms because of our own default of personal responsibility for our institutions and their operation.

Robert Heilbroner speaks of an increasing consciousness in contemporary society that "things are closing in on us," that life is becoming too complex, that the contradictions and complexities of life are making our long-term future look more and more depressing.[2] And yet he admits that on a *personal* level, he is fairly cheerful and optimistic.

His point is that all of us live on two levels; our own private lives are conducted at one level which is fairly simple and immediate, and the public events that swirl around us are conducted at quite another level. The gravity of the long-term future has very little to do with the more basic questions of our immediate lives. And, in fact, if we take the real events of those immediate lives a day at a time, we feel pretty good about things. The solution Heilbroner offers is to live our lives at the immediate level mainly and to live with fortitude and understanding in the face of dismaying public events.

I would go a step further. We must indeed understand events and trends. We must indeed demonstrate fortitude and understanding. But there is more. We must have the will to go on working for constructive change in the interests of all of our citizens. We must refuse to give in to self-pity and pessimism. We must act as though each of us can make a difference and as though we can have an impact in every area of our lives both now and in the future. Whether or not we really can have that impact is a moot question, but we sure as hell have to try because the alternative is despair.

These are difficult and frustrating times in human history. But they are also exciting times for anyone who would make a sincere attempt to minister to the needs of other humans, who would try to be less self-centered, less greedy, less self-pitying, less bitter about life. Perhaps Dag Hammarskjöld said it best some years ago in his journal:

> I don't know who—or what—put the question. I don't know when it was put. I don't even remember answering. But at some moment I did answer to someone or something "yes." And from that hour I was certain that existence is meaningful and that, therefore, my life in self-surrender had a goal.[3]

Perhaps Americans have become too jaded, too alienated, and too corrupted by objects to achieve this kind of transcendence of self. Perhaps we have lived out the days of our greatness as a society and we are on the downside of a wave of history leading to our decline or to a drastic change in the structure and texture of the technocracy we have built. That seems to be the underlying fear that has gripped us as event after event undermines our optimism and saps our predisposition to believe in our leaders and in ourselves.

And yet despite the seriousness of the events which defeat and contradict our optimism, there is the ever-present threat of the self-fulfilling prophecy. To the extent we believe that our organizations cannot be reformed and revitalized, to the extent we believe our

213

IN SEARCH OF A CORPORATE SOUL

institutions have broken down and are hopeless, we will insure that our society will be dominated by insensitive, impersonal, and dehumanizing organizations. To the extent we fail to recognize our mutual interests and our mutual needs and to work together to build a society that is responsive to the realities of the twenty-first century, we will become more and more insulated from each other and more and more alone.

Those are pretty clear challenges. The choices are also clear. Those choices are available to us now. Let us pray we choose well.

References

Chapter I

1. Alvin Toffler, *Future Shock* (New York: Random House, 1970), pp. 86–111.

2. Daniel Yankelovich, "The New Work Values—A Moving Target for Communicators," speech to the Industrial Communication Council, Princeton, N.J., October 1972.

Chapter II

1. "Crude Oil Dearth Linked to Profits" (interviews of ten oil company executives by the Associated Press), *Rochester Times-Union*, January 13, 1974.

2. John K. Galbraith, *Economics and the Public Purpose* (Boston: Houghton Mifflin, 1973), pp. 84–85.

3. David C. Anderson, "Is the Idea of Success Obsolete?" *The Wall Street Journal*, January 5, 1972.

4. Dr. Margaret Hennig, in an address to the International Association of Business Communicators, Houston, Texas, June 1973.

5. Dale Tarnowieski, *The Changing Success Ethic* (New York: AMA Survey Report, 1973).

6. Peter Chew, "Backstabbing, Inc.," *National Observer*, January 26, 1974, p. 1.

7. Peter F. Drucker, *The Effective Executive* (New York: Harper & Row, 1966) , pp. 52–70.

8. Harry Levinson, "Asinine Attitudes toward Motivation," *Harvard Business Review*, vol. 51, no. 1 (January–February 1973), pp. 70–76.

9. Frederick Herzberg, "Why Bother to Work?" *Industry Week*, July 16, 1973, pp. 46–49.

10. Adam Smith, "Last Days of Cowboy Capitalism," *The Atlantic*, September 1972, pp. 43–55.

Chapter III

1. Personal discussion with Neil Rackham, consultant to Rank Xerox, at the Xerox International Center for Training and Management Development, Leesburg, Va., August 4, 1974.

2. Harry Levinson, "Asinine Attitudes toward Motivation," *Harvard Business Review*, vol. 51, no. 1 (January–February 1973), pp. 70–76.

3. M. Scott Myers, "Conditions for Manager Motivation," *New Insights for Executive Achievement* (a compilation of *Harvard Business Review* articles, 1966), pp. 11–24.

4. Peter F. Drucker, *Management: Tasks, Responsibilities, Practices* (New York: Harper & Row, 1974), pp. 243–245.

5. Herman S. Jacobs and Katherine Jillson, *Executive Productivity* (New York: AMA Survey Report, 1974).

6. Richard Barnet and Ronald Müller, "A Reporter At Large: Multinational Corporations," *The New Yorker*, December 9, 1974, p. 156.

7. John K. Galbraith, *Economics and the Public Purpose* (Boston: Houghton Mifflin, 1973), pp. 210–212.

Chapter IV

1. Robert Townsend, *Up the Organization* (New York: Alfred A. Knopf, 1970), pp. 142–143.

2. Alexis de Tocqueville, "What Sort of Despotism Democratic Nations Have to Fear," *Democracy in America*, trans. Phillips Bradley (New York: Alfred A. Knopf, 1945).

3. Abraham H. Maslow, *Religions, Values, and Peak Experiences* (New York: Viking Press, 1964).

4. John Gardner, *The Recovery of Confidence* (New York: W. W. Norton, 1970), pp. 138–145.

5. Carol S. Gold, *Industrial Communication Newsletter,* October 1974, p. 3.

6. Gardner, *The Recovery of Confidence,* p. 140.

7. S. Terkel, "Reflections on a Course of Ethics" (interview with Jeb Stuart Magruder), *Harper's Magazine,* October 1973, pp. 59–62.

8. Joseph Heller, *Something Happened* (New York: Alfred A. Knopf, 1974), p. 67.

9. Laurence J. Peter and Raymond Hull, *The Peter Principle* (New York: William Morrow, 1969), p. xii.

10. Zbigniew Brzezinski, "Unmanifest Destiny: Where Do We Go from Here?" *New York,* March 3, 1975, pp. 51–57.

11. Colin Campbell, "Coming Apart at the Seams" (a conversation with Robert Heilbroner), *Psychology Today,* February 1975, pp. 94–103.

12. Douglas McGregor, *The Human Side of Enterprise* (New York: McGraw-Hill, 1960), pp. 232–235.

Chapter V

1. Peter F. Drucker, *Management: Tasks, Responsibilities, Practices* (New York: Harper & Row, 1974), pp. 231–235.

2. Robert F. Pearse, *Manager to Manager: What Managers Think of Management Development* (New York: AMA Survey Report, 1974), pp. 49–50.

3. Ibid, pp. 48–49.

4. Chris Argyris, "Personality vs. Organization," *Organizational Dynamics,* fall 1974, pp. 3–17.

5. William F. Dowling, "Conversation with Sir Geoffrey Vickers," *Organizational Dynamics,* fall 1974, pp. 49–64.

6. John K. Galbraith, *Economics and the Public Purpose* (Boston: Houghton Mifflin, 1973), pp. 274–285.

7. Daniel Bell, *The Coming of Post-Industrial Society* (New York: Basic Books, 1973), pp. 269–298.

8. Drucker, *Management,* pp. 809–811.

9. Alvin Toffler, *Future Shock* (New York: Random House, 1970), pp. 379–394.

10. Drucker, *Management,* p. 807.

11. Bell, *The Coming of Post-Industrial Society,* pp. 487–489.

12. Archibald MacLeish, "Freedom Is the Right to Choose," *Continuing Journey* (New York: Houghton Mifflin, 1967).

Epilogue

1. Stephen Verney, *Fire in Coventry* (Old Tappan, N.J.: Fleming H. Revell, 1965), pp. 92–95.

2. Colin Campbell, "Coming Apart at the Seams" (a conversation with Robert Heilbroner), *Psychology Today,* February 1975, pp. 94–103.

3. Dag Hammarskjöld, *Markings* (New York: Alfred A. Knopf, 1964), p. 205.